Face to Face with Practice

T0300369

Coming Face to Face with your own practice is an emerging approach to management and professional research that has a significant impact on management practice. It closes the gap between theory and practice. An existential form of research means that the researcher carefully attends to their experience of researching and managing.

This book demonstrates that by bringing an existential sensibility to research, unexpected possibilities for research and for professionality, are revealed. Each chapter shows authors grappling with the constraints of a system, navigating issues of humanness, questioning themselves, unfolding their understanding of appropriate ethics and finally, elucidating a depth of response that in itself reveals a way forward.

In *Face to Face with Practice*, authors demonstrate how they drew on moments of estrangement from their practices. They found that when such moments are respected and carefully examined, a kind of clarification and at the same time often deep disillusionment with the taken-for-granted conventions of their practice, emerge. Through exploring these conventional ways of operating, authors develop new and original accounts of what it means to manage better in their particular field of practice. Such an approach is called hermeneutic existential phenomenology, affectionately known as HEP.

Face to Face is about making a difference: a difference to the ways that management is practiced; a difference to the experience of the manager; and actually a difference towards a more humane and thoughtful approach to managing our society today.

Dr Claire Jankelson, Honorary Associate at Macquarie Graduate School of Management, Sydney, brings an enlivened engagement to teaching and researching that aims to develop leadership capacity in the learner. Further to her current practice as independent mentor and supervisor to PhD's, she is Editor-in-Chief of the *Journal of Spirituality, Leadership and Management* (JSLaM), a professional scholarly Journal that probes meaning and humanness within management practice.

Dr Steven Segal is a Senior lecturer in Management at the Macquarie Graduate School of Management. Through his range of teaching, research and publications he creates the space for students, researchers and practicing managers to develop their own theories of practice as a basis for developing practical wisdom and making a contribution to knowledge. Creating unexpected futures through research and teaching underpins his educational process.

For most people philosophy and management make an unlikely couple. Yet, as this brilliant book shows, this couldn't be more wrong: if the beginning of philosophy is wonder, the authors reflectively probe into their managerial experience, disclose their taken-for granted theories of practice and get a more lucid grasp of their own activities, prompted especially by moments of disruption and anomalies. Insofar as existential philosophy in particular illuminates experience, it ceases to be 'theoretical' and becomes intensely practical. Steve Segal and Claire Jankelson have done something rare – they show the reader how to become a philosophical practitioner. I know of no other management book that has accomplished this.

Haridimos Tsoukas, The Columbia Ship Management Professor of Strategic Management, University of Cyprus and a Distinguished Research Environment Professor of Organization Studies, University of Warwick.

This gem of a book redefines research methodology in the leadership practice. By bringing the personal into the reality of leadership the authors are changing the very nature of how we relate to our leaders and ourselves as leaders. This book is a great step in having us look at leadership in new and illuminating ways.

Margot Cairnes, Creator of 12 Steps for Business, Author of *Approaching the Corporate Heart; Peaceful Chaos and Staying Sane in a Changing World.*

Claire Jankelson and Steven Segal's Face to Face with Practice *illuminates like two lightning flashes. With the first flash, we see that innovations require personal transformations of their innovators. The second flash shows how the authors' Hermeneutic Circle enables graduate students to notice and pursue life's usually ignored, small disruptions. The book offers a path to authenticity and practical wisdom.*

Charles Spinosa, Ph.D., Group Director for Leadership Development and Customer Experience VISION Consulting

Face to Face with Practice

Existential forms of research for management inquiry

Edited by Steven Segal and Claire Jankelson

Routledge
Taylor & Francis Group

LONDON AND NEW YORK

First published 2016 by Ashgate Publishing

2 Park Square, Milton Park, Abingdon, Oxfordshire OX14 4RN
711 Third Avenue, New York, NY 10017

Routledge is an imprint of the Taylor & Francis Group, an informa business

First issued in paperback 2017

British Library Cataloguing in Publication Data
A catalogue record for this book is available from the British Library

Library of Congress Cataloging in Publication Data
A catalog record for this book has been requested

ISBN: 978-1-4724-6387-6 (hbk)
ISBN: 978-0-8153-9263-7 (pbk)

Typeset in Sabon
by Swales & Willis Ltd, Exeter, Devon, UK

Contents

Figures

Contributors

Editors

Steven Segal is a Senior Lecturer in Management at the Macquarie Graduate School of Management. Through his range of teaching, research and publications he creates the space for students, researchers and practising managers to develop their own theories of practice as a basis for developing practical wisdom and making a contribution to knowledge. Through the use of hermeneutic phenomenology as a research method he enables students to re-think their fundamental assumptions so as to create new ways of seeing, being and doing in their practice. Existential dimensions of hermeneutic phenomenology enables students to 'join the dots' of the 'dizziness' experienced in all forms of inquiry.

Claire Jankelson is an Honorary Associate at Macquarie Graduate School of Management where she supervises and has facilitated the hermeneutic circle for PhD Candidates over the past eight years. Through teaching Management and Research for decades, the core value of her teaching is in the facilitation of learning. She enjoys a particular interest in research that emerges out of one's practice and makes a difference: to practice, to the practitioner and to our world. She has an established practice as an independent Mentor and Supervisor to PhDs with a phenomenological or humanistic orientation and encourages the development of thesis writing that engages the reader. Further to a consulting practice on Thoughtful Leadership, she is Editor-in-Chief of the *Journal of Spirituality, Leadership and Management* (JSLaM), a professional scholarly journal that probes meaning and humanness within management practice.

Contributors

Rachelle Arkles joined the Centre for Health Research (CHR) at Western Sydney University in February 2016. Prior, she worked with Muru Marri at the School of Public Health and Community Medicine at UNSW Australia. Over many years, she has worked with a range of methodologies from surveys to narratives with diverse communities and population settings. Her interest and commitment to research is as a professional practice and as a form of dialogue and engagement. Her doctoral thesis addressed the experience of ageing and dementia in families of Aboriginal heritage where she explored different interpretive strategies and meanings as well as the meeting points between Indigenous philosophical perspectives and the Western research traditions of existential hermeneutic phenomenology.

Darcy Duggan spent his youth working on diesel engines and generators in the Royal Australian Navy, and then spent more than ten years in a large Australian utility company. He had various technical and management roles there, including a reprise as a change consultant. Then came a stint as a researcher for an employment services company. He now manages two grazing properties in northern New South Wales (NSW), growing beef and fine wool. He is also a doctoral candidate at Macquarie Graduate School of Management (MGSM). His interests are phenomenology, particularly the lived experience of being managed, fresh air, working dogs and the weather.

William (Bill) Hovey has headed The Linchpin Group Australia, a leading-edge consultancy noted for its work in succession in family-owned businesses in Australia, China and Europe, since 1998. His pragmatic approach integrates management practice, theory, philosophy and psychology. He is co-authoring with Dr Steven Segal a book on the existential character of leadership. He earned his BA, M Management, MBA, and MA from Macquarie University where he is currently completing his PhD in Management. His doctoral thesis emerged from his succession practice. He came to a PhD from his practice because he was puzzled by the failure of many family business owners to engage with the phenomenon of succession and he was frustrated by the limited alternatives offered by the existing models of practice.

Amanda Mead is currently a Non-Executive Director and Mentor and consults in governance, corporate strategy and change management. She is a strategist, marketer and researcher in the food and not-for-profit sectors with over 20 years' executive experience leading innovation and organisational transformation. Her research adopts a cultural perspective and explores moral emotions and identity construction in meetings during a structural organizational transformation. Her work is in the discipline of organizational behaviour, and particularly concerns integrating sociological theories of emotion and identity with management organisational change theory in practice.

Bradley Rolfe has over 20 years' experience in the delivery of technologically diverse, multi-partner, and multi-million dollar enterprise-wide infrastructure projects and programmes of work across the banking and finance, IT and telecommunications, and government sectors. Apart from his MBA, he has recently completed a doctoral thesis on the theory of project management at the MGSM. In his spare time he lectures on project management for the MBA programmes at the Sydney University Business School and the MGSM. He has also published and presented papers on project management and philosophy for a number of international journals.

Devorah Wainer is an Interdisciplinary Researcher in the arts, humanities, social and political sciences. Her research is always based on elements of her own experience. Her writing balances scholarly academic rigour with creative non-fiction and poetry. She received a place on the coveted Chancellor's List as an award for outstanding calibre doctoral scholarship for her thesis titled 'Beyond the Wire: Levinas vis-à-vis Villawood'. Her book *Beyond the Wire* (2015) remains true to the thesis, which is a study of French philosopher Emmanuel Levinas' ethics as applied to asylum-seeking refugees. She is a recognised scholar of Levinas. She developed a research methodology—the Midrash Methodology—to be congruent with his philosophy. She is an Honorary Associate in the School of Social and Political Sciences at the University of Sydney. Previously she taught ethics and communications to post-graduate students at the University of New South Wales and directed the undergraduate change management programme at UNSW for three years.

Foreword

A Philosophical Invitation

Steven Segal and Claire Jankelson

The activity of inquiring into the fundamental assumptions of one's practice is a philosophical activity. It is philosophical in the most concrete sense, and not in the unfortunate common sense understanding of philosophy as the study of abstractions.

Karl Lewin once said that there is nothing more practical than a good theory. A theory gives us perspective. It is like the light that allows us to see things although we do not see the very light itself. Theory gives us an appreciation of the rules of the game that we are playing. If we do not have an appreciation of the rules of the game that we are playing, we cannot make sense of the rules of the game. We simply do not know how to play.

The virtue of a theory is that it is already, for the most part, in the background of our practice. When playing a game, we should not need to spend too much time thinking about the rules of the game in order to play the game effectively. Indeed, the more we spend time thinking about the rules of the game, the less attentive we are to the trajectory of the ball and so before we know it, the ball has passed us by.

Thomas Kuhn, the father of the modern use of the word *paradigm*, said that a scientist should not need to spend too much time thinking about their paradigm. It gets in the way of their everyday activities as a scientist. Scientists need to take the rules of their game for granted in order to play it effectively – as does a sportswomen or man.

Kuhn says that it is only in times of paradigm crisis that scientists are challenged to think through the rules of the scientific game that they are playing. And thereby they unknowingly and unwittingly become philosophers. He and many others say: Philosophy is the activity of questioning the rules of the game that we are playing.

However, it is a special sort of questioning of the rules. It is a questioning of the rules in the life world of the scientist. This means that it is not just a questioning of an abstract set of principles. It is much more fundamental than that. It is a questioning of the rules in the context of playing by the rules! It is a questioning of the very fundamental basis upon which the scientist makes sense of the world. It is a questioning of the very rules that have up until this point, guided the scientist and their way of doing science. These rules have formed the basis of the security of the scientist, and of her or his identity.

When these rules are thrown into question, the scientist may find themselves in a vortex of deep anxiety. Thomas Kuhn gives Albert Einstein, Niels Bohr, Heisenberg and Wolfgang Pauli, those fathers of modern science, as exemplars of people who have had the fundamental rules of the scientific game knocked out of them. They have been thrust into deep uncertainty in order to finally disclose the world in new and different ways. Einstein disclosed the world of relativity and Heisenberg and Bohr opened up the world of quantum physics. Each of them experienced the collapse of the old scientific conventions and, through bringing deep thoughtfulness, new forms emerged.

For most of their lives they were scientists. At crucial periods they became philosophers. And when they became philosophers they came face to face with their own practice as scientists. And this coming face to face was frightening and created a sense of vulnerability. In time it also created the courage of authenticity, of authoring their own work and, in that space, disclosing whole new fields of inquiry.

This book focuses on the way in which such paradigm crises are opportunities for becoming philosophers in-practice. What will be seen in the pages that follow are a group of managers who have become philosophical practitioners through a process of working through 'paradigm crises' in the context of their professional practices. Through the working-through of a paradigm crisis, they have each developed new or broader worlds of practice by examining their taken-for-granted theories of practice. This experience enabled them to develop the competencies for working on their practice while staying within their practices. They have developed the competencies or ways of being to become philosophical management practitioners.

We are asking you the reader to be open to a new meaning of the practice of philosophy; one in which philosophy is not simply an abstract set of propositions to be analyzed but one through which philosophy enables professionalism. Through each and every chapter of the book we are offering you the possibility to see a process of reinventing a practice, a methodology, even ways of living.

Philosophical research offers a generic set of reflective and reflexive competencies for staying tuned in the twenty-first century. The capacity for responding to paradigm crises is essential for coping in a world of qualitative uncertainty; a world in which our lives seem stable but suddenly without warning, our very practices seem to shatter. This experience is almost commonplace. Like a fish that swims in water, we are seldom aware of the theories in which we swim. It takes much thoughtful and challenging inquiry to become aware of the theory of practice that has guided and shaped our ways of being and doing in our practices. And then slowly, there is the opportunity to rebuild our practice, differently; more coherently suited to what the practice needs.

Experiential philosophy – or more particularly existential philosophy – is that form of research which provides a framework for making explicit the *implicit* and the *taken-for-granted* theory or *set of conventions* which guide our own practice.

Research regarding our own theories of practice is experiential because we are inquiring into our ways of doing things. It is philosophical because we are exploring our assumptions. And we are using our lived experience of being in doubt, troubled and even anxious as opportunities through which to explore the assumptions of our practice. Furthermore, we are opening up new ways of being in practice.

In existential–experiential forms of research, we are ourselves part of the research. Such experience or existential forms of philosophizing are actually a research novelty. Traditional social scientific management research is guided by principles of science. Axiomatic to science is a separation between the researcher and the researched, the thinker and the doer. These stand at an objective distance from each other.

The psychologist Carl Rogers once said that what is most personal is also most universal. Each author in this book is a professional who is provoked by something 'troubling' in their practice. This is not research for the sake of doing research. Rather it is research that arises out of deep care and concern for the particular area of inquiry, often after many years of professional practice. Each one of the authors is both courageous and authentic in how they bring their particular voice to their inquiring, their research, their understanding and their expression of what transpired in the process.

When through moments of interruptions in our lived experience we inquire into the assumptions that guide our actions, we are entering into a process of philosophizing.

Many may ask: what makes this research? And the answer is very simple: it is through the exploration of the lived experiences of particular practices that general assumptions emerge: assumptions which are neither yours nor mine but ours.

All of the chapters of this book invite you to do more than read and absorb the work of the authors; they call you to explore your own taken-for-granted theories of practice and thereby to enter into the lived experience of your own philosophical activity.

Introduction

Claire Jankelson and Steven Segal

This book has been more than seven years in the making. Over this period, each one of the authors has developed a particular attunement within their fields of professionalism and research. This book offers examples of practitioners who have used their professional engagement as the springboard for inquiring into their practices.

Each chapter offers a different story of transformation. Each story takes the form of reflective and reflexive inquiry into the lived experience of the practitioner. These are case studies from a broad range of engagements; some more organizationally orientated and others are more socially orientated. Each one has to do with how the authors' voices emerge through the process of inquiry, their authoring or authentication. And this is what gives the writing flavour. The chapters are both personal and impersonal, they are subjective and objective, they are subtle and nuanced and often give the reader an experience in reading. They are practice orientated and yet overlaid and immersed within theory. Yet each has significant practical consequences and implications.

This book follows themes from the recently published book *Management Practice and Creative Destruction* by Steven Segal. In that book the grounds for developing a hermeneutic, existential and phenomenological (HEP) approach to Higher Degrees Research in Management were outlined and exemplified. It claimed that very little research and writing had been undertaken on the existential dimensions of management. It was noted that while HEP as an approach to research had found its way into psychology, nursing and education as professional practices, it had not yet found its way into management as a practice or profession. The book clearly demonstrated the significance and value of HEP for management inquiry, research, education and practice.

An overarching feature of this book is that each chapter offers *practitioner* research. This implies that the authors' roles as professionals are interconnected with their research conducted. Practices have been reshaped as a result of research findings. This means, that unlike most research, the issues emerge out of an area of the practitioner's concern and the outcomes of the research offer new ways of being in practice.

The series of chapters exemplify what occurs when HEP is used as a framework for research in the practice of management and other areas. They show how a HEP perspective opens up a field of inquiry and a way of thinking-through that is not possible within most research approaches.

Contrasting a HEP approach with a traditional positivist and Cartesian form of research helps to show up the nuances of the HEP approach. Positivist forms of science and research build a clear distinction between the researcher and the content of what is researched. The researcher stands at a neutral and objective distance from the subject. The methods of research used to collect data are employed in such a way as to eliminate bias. The methodologies used to analyze the data aim towards an objective 'answer' to the research question. The researcher will wish to be able to represent the facts of the situation as they are, through being methodologically precise. A positivist approach aims towards a particular notion of truth where the researcher writes or represents the state of affairs corresponding to only that which can be *seen* and *heard*. This correspondence theory of truth makes subject and object into two ontologically distinct substances. Further experiences that cannot be put in the form of visible or quantifiable objects do not qualify as subject matter worthy of research. And this framework therefore excludes the entire category of the *lived experience* of the professional or manager.

Lived experience is at the core of the work in this book. For management is all about people and people are immersed in their experience. But, for the most part managers are not educated in the art and discipline of learning to read experience. Management education is generally based on analyzing data and not on reading what Mintzberg (2004) calls *firsthand experience*. Quoting a CEO, Mintzberg (2004) demonstrates that learning to read experience is an art or discipline in its own right: 'My problem is that when I face a problem, I don't know what class I am in.' Mintzberg is therefore suggesting that managers need to learn to read the challenge of their experience that they find themselves within and that this necessary capacity is integral in responding to it effectively. One of the primary focuses of HEP is learning to name experience so as to deal with *lived experience*. The work draws on notions of *felt sense* and *focusing* from Eugene Gendlin (1981) as a basis of enabling managers to name their experiences and, in the context of this book, to name their ways of inquiring.

A HEP approach means that researchers do not shy away from the emotions, feelings and values that have led them to make their inquiries. It is relatively rare to hear of researchers naming the nuances of the experience of conducting their research. Indeed the thrust of most research is to achieve the objectivity and single mindedness of research that dismisses the presence of the researcher completely and thereby can answer a research question without any confounding variables. In this work, the experience of the researcher is intrinsically connected with and impactful on the progress, the shaping and the outcomes of the research. And many would ask why this experience is significant or important?

What each of these authors are researching is part of who they are or their very *way of being* in their practices. The reader will notice that there is a kind of courage that arises through coming face to face with their fields of inquiry and, as Brene Brown (2012) points out, moral courage emerges when people speak their heart. This requires the practitioner researcher to develop a kind of attentiveness or mindfulness about their practice. The resulting research that unfolds is not so much about driving and following a research question; it is about holding a point of focus through which new perspectives can arise! We call this openness to new perspectives in research, phenomenology. The result is that the researcher develops an attunement within their area of research and thereby to their practices. This will be clearly seen in practice in the chapters that follow.

Background

Steven Segal and Claire Jankelson have co-facilitated seven years of supervising PhDs within a hermeneutic circle context. These PhD candidates, most of whom have since completed their doctoral dissertations, are professionals at the Macquarie Graduate School of Management, Sydney, Australia. The circle was a great opportunity to learn about research while doing research: it involved inquiring about arising questions and research issues, reflecting on these issues whilst being with the experience of the issues. The approach recognizes that knowledge does not exist apart from experience but is rather a dialectic and dynamic relationship with a circular rhythm. Certainly learning arises through gaining experience and reflecting on experience. Knowing something becomes possible through the learning from and the reflecting on experience.

Knowledge itself can be considered clear cut. Experience comes to us as a complex and often messy business. The process of gaining knowledge or understanding from experience can be said to be the action of researching or inquiring. Peter Willis (2000: 23) suggests that ' . . . professional practice without personal engagement is alienating and ultimately irresponsible' and similarly inquiring into one's practice inclusive of personal engagement can be said to be responsible and perhaps, ethical action. Our experience as supervisors has shown the hermeneutic circle dialogue process to be an effective cultivation of the capacity for researching (see Chapter 1 for a detailed description of the hermeneutic circle).

From Practice to Research

The research in this book is about *coming face to face*: face to face with oneself within one's practices, as one is researching one's practice. And this is what one means by *being* in the research rather than removing oneself from the context of the research. Furthermore, *being-in* research is still not enough for coming face to face with one's practice of research. As Heidegger (1962) points out, the lived experience of coming face to face with one's way of *being-in* practice presupposes moments of estrangement from one's practice. In such moments one is simultaneously in one's practice and observing oneself being in one's practice. This is the heart of existentialism. And from the existential perspective, it is the heart of what it means to be human. Whilst we know such an experience well, we seldom have the language to describe this experience.

We refer to the authors as managers in the sense of both an organizational role and also a very generic sense of *managing*. Each chapter is concerned with people and the researcher's engagement with those people. The focus is on the way of being a manager in context and not on the formal role of manager.

Each chapter is a sensitive inquiry into a subject of significance to the inquirer. The subject matter has emerged out of the author's life work or area of care and concern. Each author is a researcher and a professional. The authors as researchers recognize their impacts on their subject matter and value the depth that such a penetration offers. Each works with reflection and with reflexivity within a carefully formulated methodological inquiry.

Researching as Hermeneutic Existential Phenomenological (HEP)

Researching as inquiry can be seen as a whole process. It has many parts within the process and each of those parts is both a reflection of and a shaping of the whole of the research inquiry. HEP research recognizes that the researcher is both whole and one of those parts and how they bring themselves to the research in turn shapes and directs what is found. This is a form of inquiry in which (the boundaries between) the researcher's relationship with the work, the methodology for doing research, what counts as 'data', even theorizing itself is all emergent and is actually shaped through the doing of the research. The whole and its parts are in a dynamic relationship and whilst there are frequent moments of the experience of 'getting lost' in the research, actually that disruption or confusion will hold the clues for new insight. The commonplace impartiality of the research scientist where the researcher and the subject matter are separated in an objective relationship is anathema to this schema and can be found in countless books in management bookshops. What you'll find in this book are a series of extraordinary stories: stories that matter, life stories, crisis stories, disruptive stories. Each one is impressive and expressive.

Hermeneutic

The hermeneutic aspect of research involves the coming face to face with one's usual practices, also called the conventions of practice. And coming face to face is not an exaggeration of what transpires. This researcher is not reviewing their practice as something that is separate from him or herself. The researcher is inquiring from within their living experience of their conventions; examining their practice from within (what he or she is already within). This is a process of recognizing the usual assumptions and the usual ways of operating that have been the conventions of practice. The coming face to face with one's practice is an experience of deep questioning. In coming to grips with this experience, the researcher will cast off or empty out or bracket the usual ways of accumulating knowledge and the usual ways of being or practicing.

Lived Experience as Truth

Supported by Aristotelian and different HEP philosophies, management is treated neither as an object nor as a subject but as the lived experience of a relationship between beings. At times, these beings are subjects and at other time objects, however the truth is more like a qualitative network of living and shifting relationships. Heidegger (1985: 155) suggests that we 'find ourselves' amidst our involvements in the world.

Truth, as a kind of goal or intention, from a HEP perspective is about vision, about seeing and noticing anew. It is closer to insight than it is to knowledge or a new fact. It is concerned with disclosing new worlds or new ways of being within the world. Shotter quotes Taptiklis speaking about Tom Peters: 'What was striking about Peters was that he demonstrated enormous curiosity about the everyday life of the organizations . . . he wanted to get inside and even immerse himself in organizational life. Most of all he wanted managers to notice things' (1985: 85). Noticing anew is the essence of HEP.

HEP makes *lived experience* the very centre of concern and study. We suggest that management is primarily a *lived experience*: it takes place in time, in contextual or historical conditions, under conditions in which managers are confronted with choice in the context of action, where their way of being or doing things is at stake and requires continuous concern or engagement.

This form of research aims to improve professional practice, to open up new ways of being a practitioner and to enable novice professionals to learn from the experience of previous practitioners who have written up their practice in disciplined and rigorous ways. This is sharply contrasted with the multitude of popular biographies of leaders or other professionals who make idealistic claims about their practices.

Hermeneutic Existential Phenomenological (HEP) as Practitioner Orientated Research

HEP is always a practitioner orientated process of researching and focuses on forms of inquiry that can transpire from being within a practice. And sometimes, as will be seen in many of the chapters in this book, it is actually the practice itself that 'draws' one in. As Heidegger (1985) suggests when things are on course, there is no need to do research. It is when our work goes off course, is interrupted or disrupted in some form that research solicits and summons.

A rich example of this in the world of management can be seen in the work of Fernando Flores (1982), the founder of a management practice called 'Conversations for Action'. In the midst of his practice he began to notice something that was quite unexpected and strange. Based on his job description, he expected to be developing sets of town plans but in practice he noticed that he spent most of his time in conversation with people. He experienced this as a strange contradiction. Now, rather than attempting to resolve the contradiction, he continued observing his way *of being* in the contradiction and the more he observed his way of being in contradiction, the more fascinated he became by it. Through staying with this contradictory state of things, he came to see that conversations rather than formal planning was the central role of his activity as a manager. So excited was he with this that he enrolled for a PhD on the role of conversations which when completed in 1982 was called *Management and Communication in the Office of the Future. It* became the basis of a very successful consultancy practice.

Some of the main principles of HEP can be noted in his research process. He was drawn into a reflexive relationship to his practice by an anomaly or disruption in his practice (existentialism). Because he was sensitive to this phenomenon, he could simultaneously dwell in and observe himself in contradiction. He was drawn to his actual lived experience (phenomenology). The more he was able to dwell within the contradiction, the more he was able to reframe – or more precisely – he could re-gestalt his practice as a manager (hermeneutics). What had been the whole of his role became a part and his sense of the whole of his role was changed such that he began to see his role in a very different way. His practice was thereby reframed. He developed his understanding of his actual role. And from being the person who controlled the way in which plans were made he was now able to clearly see that he was actually holding effective conversations for action. The very conventions of his role as manager were altered. And the practice itself has been reconfigured. He was able to see his practice anew.

The hermeneutic nature of research involves both the coming face to face with one's conventions and the re-gestalting of practice. There is no subject looking at an object. Both these defining aspects of hermeneutics are significant. Coming face to face with one's practice means that the taken for granted ways of being-in-convention become explicit. And secondly the relationship between the whole and parts of management practice is reconstituted!

A second useful example is the experience of Steven Johnson when appointed as CEO of Fox studios. In the shower, preparing for his first day as CEO of Fox studios he was struck by the question: what does a CEO actually do? He had no doubt that both his formal education and his organizational experience had prepared him for the position and yet he found himself floundering in his attempt to answer this question. Eventually after many attempts and even asking his wife's opinion, he could not answer this question and he realized that he had lost all idea of what it means to be a leader or CEO. It was in precisely this moment of acceptance of his inability that he recognized the value of raising the *question* of what it means to be a leader. And this set him off on a path of experiencing both his own history of leadership experience as well as others whom he came to identify as leaders. Out of this researching came a book on the meaning of leadership.

It was in the context of practice, of his new job role, that he came to question his own way of being in practice. His actual conventions for practice became explicit through the experience of being estranged from his practice. His conventions did not emerge as scientific objects of thought. Rather his way of being-in-convention emerged as provocative of thought. Clearly, the question is neither about what is outside of us nor about what is inside of us but what we are already within. This is the meaning of attunement with hermeneutic questioning for we are questioning the very conventions through which we make sense of our world. Heidegger says the roles we play show that we are *always and already* within a set of conventions: mother, father, professional, child, partner, divorcee etc. Paradoxically, suggests Heidegger, the set of conventions and roles are often blind to us. We do not see them while we are in them and yet they form the background of our actions, guiding whatever we do, how we relate, judge, make decisions, think and see. They come to the foreground at times of difficulty or crisis.

It is in moments of existential threat to or estrangement from a convention that a person then stands both inside and outside of their practice. Hubert Dreyfus (1993) gives the example of the distance that people stand from each other in different cultural conventions. In our own culture, we do not notice the conventions for standing close together or far apart. We may find ourselves feeling uneasy when a person stands too close or too far. And in this moment we are able to see both our own and the others' conventions for doing things. Similarly we can think of the cultural practice of using first or second names on first occasions of meeting. Our awareness of our convention arises when confronted by experiencing the unease of a different convention.

The human being is such that they can simultaneously be doing something while watching themselves doing those things. Existential authors like Douglas Mullen have argued that this is a feature peculiar to human beings. The process of being able to observe or watch ourselves while doing things is a process in which the lived experience of our being-in-convention begins to be revealed to us.

For Heidegger, questioning is not primarily a cognitive activity. It involves the whole being of a person. Heidegger expresses this by saying that questioning emerges out of the way in which our being-in-the-world is *in question*. And this occurs in moments of estrangement from our ways of being. This represents a breakdown in the familiar or felt sense of our habits of practice.

We'd like to invite you the reader to enjoy, learn from and engage with the chapters in this book. Each one is a reflexive form of research that uses experience as the basis upon which to improve or liberate oneself from constraining conventions, to innovate and disclose new possibilities. You will notice that the research is less an intentional observation of practice than it is a playful kind of watching and waiting for the way in which the *always and already*, the *average everyday* or the *conventions of practice* emerge. This is an opportunity to examine them, re-describe them and thereby to liberate oneself; to open up new possibilities for being in the world; and ultimately to make the world a better place; a safer place!

Claire Jankelson

Towards Phronesis: The Hermeneutic Circle as a Lived Experience of Research

This chapter offers a narrative description of the author's experience demonstrating how researchers find their voices and their leadership in their research through the dialogue occurring in a hermeneutic circle of supervision. Central to this process is working with the vulnerable moments in research for such moments enable researchers to become attuned to their research. The emergent themes include the cultivation of practice, grappling and uncertainty, relationship and dialogue, playfulness and humour. The outcome of the Hermeneutic Circle experience is correlated with the Aristotelian notion of phronesis – roughly translated as 'practical wisdom'. The chapter explores the nature of how phronesis could be understood to be occurring for PhD candidates through participation in the circle within each of their roles as managers within their practices, as researchers with a PhD candidature and within a Higher Education field. An assumption of HEP is that there are times in the process of research that the researcher is thrown off track, especially and not only for a novice researcher. The chapter is written in such a way that the reader may be able to replicate such an environment and thereby enable a similar learning environment.

Darcy Duggan

Stuck between Management Theory and a Hard Place: The Lived Experience of Managing in the Space between Senior Management and the Real World

This chapter tells the story of a senior manager caught in the conundrum of the expectations of the role of being a manager and his better judgement, set against the backdrop of an organization balancing the discrepancy between how it represents its operations and its actual performance. Initially Darcy was simply perplexed by what he perceived as frequent illogical practices that he and some of his work colleagues began to refer to as 'stupiding'. Darcy undertook an exploration of this phenomenon as the basis of his PhD research. Through his exploration of *stupiding*, he came to contextualize the notion of *stupiding* in the work of Thomas Kuhn and other organizational theorists who refer to this phenomenon as anomaly. *Anomaly* became the pivotal opportunity for revising and reconceptualizing the life of the organization. Darcy had the unique opportunity to carry out research based on finding the positive value of the series of anomalies and presenting his findings to the organization in the context of a conversation.

Amanda Mead and Steven Segal

Moments of Resolve: Existential Challenges of Everyday Working Life

This chapter makes a seldom addressed and yet common sense claim: it is through those small but significant everyday experiences that managers build their identity. It is an anomaly that the lived experiences of managers are seldom noticed and yet it is those very universal moments that offer themselves daily for managerial identity formation or *becoming a manager*. The chapter shows how HEP creates the space for identifying and working with these almost imperceptible moments. The story is contextualized within the emotionally labile environment of a merger and acquisition where one of the authors, Amanda, is confronted and finds a response that deeply affirms her way of being as a manager. Such events become significant for the ontological security of management.

Brad Rolfe

Escaping the Iron Triangle: Existential Hermeneutics and the Practice of Project Management

In this chapter, Brad demonstrates how he managed to emancipate himself from the traditional conventions of project management. He tells the story of how initially he was not aware that he was acting from within particular conventions of practice: he was simply doing his job! And therefore when his doubts arose in his practice as a project manager, he interpreted these doubts as his own shortcomings or his incapacity as a project manager. In response to this Brad did a number of courses on formal project management in order to improve his capacity. However none of these courses relieved his sense of doubt about his work. Eventually, through staying with his desperation, Brad began to recognize that the doubts were less about his capacity to cope than they were about the established conventions of the practice of project management. He was able to see his doubts in new ways and to recognize that the failure that he had been experiencing and attributing to himself was actually a contradiction within the conventions of project management. Through applying a HEP methodology, Brad discloses a new way of seeing, doing and being in project management. He draws on a philosophical sensibility to redefine his doubts, refine his understanding of the limitations of current project management practice and to shape up a hermeneutic approach to project management.

Rachelle Arkles

Finding My Researcher Voice: From Disorientation to Embodied Practice

The lived experience of research practice is at the core of this research as Rachelle as researcher confronts unexpected responses and even disorientation in her meeting with 'interviewees'. This chapter offers a HEP application to issues of political and social justice where, in the bid to develop an understanding of the phenomenon, the experience of dementia for Aboriginal people, the chapter argues for the essential value of the implicit experience of the researcher. This preconceptual dimension of experience becomes the fundamental resource for 'data' analysis and for researcher sense making. As the experience of the inquiry is described so does a kind of portal into the phenomenon begin to be disclosed. The vehicle of learning is thus driven by the ontological understanding that arises from the practice of research as reflexive, with all its contradictions, uncertainties and opportunities for sense making. Insight emerges with the recognition of how each individual story is set within a wider historical narrative; the limited availability of information about the experience of Aboriginal family carers for elders with dementia; the entanglement of being a researcher within conflicted narratives.

Bill Hovey

Being-in-Practice: Making the Leap from the Instrumental Technocratic to an Existential Hermeneutic Practice in Family Business Succession Consulting

This chapter shows how an entire practice of consulting in succession planning was recreated through an exploration of a meaningful critical incident. Like most other succession planners, Bill initially ran his practice attending to the traditional transactional dimensions of succession including the practices of accounting and legal matters. Through the disruption of a client's life threatening incident, Bill came to recognize that succession involved a qualitatively different dimension from those instrumental ways of operating. He shows how effective succession planning requires managing and resolving issues of meaningful significance such as purpose, legacy and relationships. Effective resolution implied new ways of being in the world for his clients. Crucial to Bill's process is that he now situates the instrumental approach within the context of an existential attunement. And he offers pathways for succession planners to broaden their horizons and go beyond an instrumental approach.

Devorah Wainer

Midrash Methodology

Devorah offers an approach to researching and research writing that fully attends to an I-thou nature of the meeting of researcher, the researched and the reader. Is this even possible whilst still meeting appropriate academic standards?

This research story is set within a current human rights issue of our times: the world of the asylum seeker. The work carries with care the concomitant challenge to recognize the ethical act of inquiring without further objectifying the researchee. Drawing on a Levinas hermeneutic methodology, Devorah as researcher approaches the subject of her research with the interest of who the subject is and what is behind what they are saying. This is not research that has the pursuit of knowledge as its goal. The goal of the midrash methodology is to invite the reader to enter the world that the text discloses and to dialogue with it themselves. At the intersection of the midrash, the author–researcher and the listener–reader is interpretation. This reflexive researcher story engages the reader into the very voices of the asylum seekers. The writings of the methodology thereby blend with the writings of the findings; as lived experience of the author. The writing is thereby reflexive and poetic and engaging.

References

Bortoft, H, 1996, *The Wholeness of Nature: Goethe's Way of Science*, Edinburgh: Floris Books.

Brown, B, 2012, *Daring Greatly: How the Courage to Be Vulnerable Transforms the Way We Live, Love, Parent, and Lead*, New York: Gotham Books.

Flores, F, 1982, *Management and Communication in the Office of the Future*, Berkley, CA: University of California.

Gendlin, E, 1981, *Focusing*, New York: Bantam Books.

Heidegger, M, 1985, *Being and Time*, Oxford: Blackwell.

Dreyfus, H, 1993, Heidegger on the Connection between Nihilism, Art Technology, and Politics. in *The Cambridge Companion to Heidegger*, edited by C. Guignon. Cambridge: Cambridge University Press.

Mintzberg, H, 2004, *Managers: Not MBAs: A Hard Look at the Soft Practice of Managing and Management Development*, San Francisco: Berret Koehler Publishers.

Shotter, J, 1985, Adopting a Process Orientation . . . in Practice: Chiasmic Relations, Language, and Embodiment in a Living World, in *Process, Sensemaking, and Organizing*, edited by T Hernes and S Maitlis. Perspectives on Process Organization Studies, Oxford: OUP.

Willis, P, Smith, R, Collins, E, (Eds) 2000, *Being, Seeking, Telling: Expressive Approaches to Qualitative Adult Education Research*, Queensland, Australia: Post Pressed.

Chapter 1

Towards Phronesis

The Hermeneutic Circle as a Lived Experience of Research[1]

Claire Jankelson

Introduction

This chapter aims to showcase the application of a hermeneutic phenomenological approach, a Hermeneutic Circle, to working with professionals doing their PhDs and learning about research. With the learning situated in a Graduate Management School, comes the recognition that this work is operating within Higher Education, Research and Management and it is at the confluence of each of these areas that the manifestation of phronesis as the lived experience of practical wisdom will be sought.

The goal for the Hermeneutic Circle (hereafter called the Circle) is to stimulate the practice of the art and craft of embodied and contextualized research. In this context, research itself becomes a practice and lived experience as the group grapple with making sense of, understanding and interpreting the practice of PhD research.

It is hoped that the reader will appreciate the practice, the complexity and the value of the Circle, and perhaps through this detailed description, be able to operationalize an equivalent environment or practice. The actual writing of this chapter will use tools of expression which suggest the action of a hermeneutic circle; the narrative weaves between description, reflection, action and silence in all possible orders. The case study situates a description of the Circle as it has evolved through a seven-year cycle and names the events of the Circle and the experience and intentions of this author (and supervisor participant). Following the description are some of the overarching themes that clearly arise from reflecting on the case. It will be noted that these emergent themes cohere with the descriptors of phronesis that follow.

The two primary thinkers on hermeneutic phenomenology, Heidegger and Gadamer, had a particular interest in phronesis. Both describe and directly connect their theories with Aristotelian phronesis and compare 'practical wisdom' with Aristotle's other types of wisdom (Bernstein 1988; Palmer 1969).

The Circle can usefully be considered as creating the conditions for actual understanding to occur. Within this space, methods such as dialogic

---

1 Parts of this chapter have been used with permission from Gower UK from a chapter by the same author found in *A Handbook of Practical Wisdom*, edited by W Kupers and D J Pauleen, England: Gower, 47–63.

engagement become a practice for accessing the pre-conceptual under-pinnings of participants' experience. Through the group engagement the access to these research underpinnings offer the scope for the arising phenomenon to access a larger concept, thereby using the parts to get to the whole and the whole as a way of accessing the particularity of a concept. This is a dialectic process of recognizing how the whole contextualizes each of the parts in the process of continuously seeking to illuminate the phenomenon within its context (Higgs et al. 2012). Through this herme-neutic practice, preconceptions emerge and genuine understanding and interpretation is reached. The circle-like nature is an essential aspect of enabling the understanding! And the notion of understanding, as experi-ence, impassions and helps shape direction in research. It's apt to remember that whilst the Circle is called a hermeneutic circle, 'it is not to be reduced to the level of a vicious circle, or even a circle which is merely tolerated' (Heidegger 1962, section 32). Indeed, it is through the circularity that the illumination occurs.

The Circle is situated within a management school at a university in Sydney, Australia. The participants are PhD candidates and two super-visors.[2] This study focuses on the practice of research rather than the theoretical development of research, management and learning within Higher Education. Each of these areas can be seen as a practice where the idea of practice is not defined simply in relation to the distinction of theory versus practice; or a particular set of rules. Instead, practice is closer to the Greek term praxis, which refers to human activity as a member of the society. As Coulter and Wiens (2002) describe, praxis demands a particular kind of engaged, embodied and enacted judgement that links knowledge, virtue and reason. Praxis can therefore be characterized as trying to act in the best way possible within the particular circumstances. Phronesis as the lived experience of practical wisdom is integrally connected with praxis: a practice that goes beyond rules, that deliberates and takes all possible circumstances into account in order to do one's best (Kemmis 2011). Kemmis describes how phronesis arises out of praxis as the wisdom that emerges out of experience.

What is the nature of the knowledge or the knowing that emerges through the engagement within the Circle and how can it be said to be useful or add value for management candidates engaged in their PhD research? What is the nature of the dialogue between the candidates and how is this dialogue significant to the individual candidate and to the supervisors? When can one speak of a lived experience of phronesis occurring and how would such

2 The other supervisor is Dr Steven Segal, a senior lecturer at the University and co-editor of this book. Together we conceived, developed and facilitated The Hermeneutic Circle as a method for effective supervision and research practice.

an occasion be identifiable? These are the questions that this chapter is a consideration of and response to.

The chapter concludes with some reflections on the value of phronesis as a framework to evaluate the Circle. It offers pointers about the movement of this chapter as both transparently expressing the art and practice of phronesis and the Circle as *phronesis-in-action*. Finally it reviews the generalizability of the work of the Circle in relation to the applicability of such a methodology to other practices, including within management and Higher Education.

Narrative Description of the Circle

The two supervisors who created the Circle have been teaching in academic institutions for decades, and have a keen interest in the educational and management learning opportunities that doing Higher Degree Research in a management school can provide. One supervisor had been director of Higher Degree Research and the other supervisor and author of this chapter had completed her own PhD a number of years earlier with the inspirational support of a small group of three PhD candidates who met regularly and dialogued using a Bohmian-style[3] conversation.

There was no blueprint for how this research circle would proceed. We were both anxious and excited at the idea of innovating a new form of learning within an academic institution, of offering PhD candidates another supervision option. In preparation for first creating the Circle, the supervisors held conversations with one another and immersed ourselves in the theory and practice of hermeneutics. Recognizing that researching itself is intrinsically an extension of the researcher, we wanted to create an environment in which the drawing forth of intentionality and even methodology could transpire. It appeared that a hermeneutic phenomenological theoretical framework could support the intentions of reflecting on, learning and drawing out the phronesis of researchers in the context of lived experience?

We had recognized how 'lost' many PhD candidates appeared. They had lost their direction and engagement. We believed that that emotion of 'feeling lost' often contains the seeds that could be transformative to their research process. We knew that transformation can occur from learning how to be in question with your questions: a kind of embracing of that 'lostness'. The core idea was that research itself is a lived experience or practice that requires a particular kind of perception and practice to

---

3 This refers to a form of dialogue which is non-hierarchical, a moment of silence is practised between speakers; communication is self-directed in an inquiring rather than an advocating style whilst listening is paramount (Bohm 1990).

manage. We believed that a 'good' research practice could translate into having a consequential PhD experience that may have an impact both on the research process and on candidates' professional management practices.

The possibilities of such a conversation excited us as supervisors. Having myself conducted extensive research and taught the art and craft of research, I suspected that the group intelligence could offer a kind of window or extra perspective that is unattainable by any other means. I felt challenged to nurture my perceptual, facilitatory and group communication skills that would enable each person's research practice to flourish.

Sessions are scheduled as monthly afternoon events. This frequency has continued and appears to be a good interval between sessions. Most of our candidates are professional management practitioners who are working either full or part time. The time they give up for the supervision group is considered precious and there have been challenges from candidates with regard to the group time being used for optimal results. Attendance at the group is completely voluntary.

From 12 to 15 mature age people are seated around a boardroom table, including the supervisors. The split of males to females is roughly equal. The mode of operating is respectful and friendly. As supervisors, we have created a plan and intention for structuring the session. This may include individual presentation, a group writing or exercise such as reflection on progress and problems experienced.

We reiterate our intention, which is to create an environment within which candidates can 'be in' the practice of research and that it is from this experience of 'being-in' that the question or the phenomenon develops. This is the basis for reflecting upon and theorizing the research process. As supervisors, we agree on most pedagogical and philosophical principles. Our disagreements often concern the relative amounts of time given for presentation and academic content compared with a more spontaneous or off-the-cuff type inquiry. The third hidden role in our disagreement is the academic institution. It calls for measurable outcomes and appropriate theorizing. What constitutes a 'good enough' session may be different for the three parties. We communicate openly with the group and with one another in deciding to change or reshape the direction the group is moving through.

It is complex to try to delineate the method that is used to facilitate the conversation. To call it a method is to lock it into a set of rules and procedures and yet it is so much more than that – there is no order to what we do – there is a dynamic responsiveness and attempt at sensitivity to what is unfolding by the group. We are often surprised at what actually transpires in the group. The most I can offer are a number of pointers that signify what we may do. I believe that were this piece to be written by the other supervisor or by the students themselves, they may describe something quite different.

Presentations in the Circle are encouraged to be on topics in progress or on topics that candidates are grappling with. Presentations may be methodological, related to actual content or on a topic related to the experience of doing research. Sometimes students use the session to hone their ideas as practice in anticipation of a more formal presentation.

Candidates drive their own presentation process by inviting questions and conversation. The group listens carefully with full attention. We listen for what has not been said, for what is perhaps missing. We listen for an internal logic and flow, for the resonance between the presenter and the content of their presentation. We listen for what the phenomenon is that is just behind or within the content; perhaps this is the context that is driving the content. Questions and comments build towards a shared understanding through the group interaction and collaboration. Connections are uncovered and discovered: these could be resonances of topics between candidates; applications to the Weltanschauung or the Zeitgeist; academic literature sources that support or contradict; archetypal or mythical connections.

As supervisors, we are both gatekeepers and drivers of the conversation. We are mindful of content and the nature of the relationships within the group, the irritations and the power play. We make an effort to keep bringing the conversation back to the details of the actual experience of what is being described. This may include: questioning the meaning of what is being stated; reaching into understanding the nature of what is described; noticing connections or similarities between speakers; fine tuning the theorizing; framing what is said in theory; appreciating the breadth and depth of the words and meanings and bringing this to attention; and seeking the context or background of what is described.

We are cultivating a mindful practice: the appreciation of what is arising. Avoiding finding solutions or answers sometimes feels like trying to keep the door open when the wind is blowing hard. Perhaps the wind is the academic tradition that insists on closure, on finding answers, of compartmentalizing theory and practice. I notice my own tendencies to judge, to interpret and to 'dismiss' a phenomenon by theorizing. The kinds of question that I often bring into my consciousness and sometimes share with the group include: what are we now learning or understanding about research? What does it mean to 'stand in' the phenomenon that is being spoken about? What else is being said here? What is underlying all of this?

Sometimes a particular kind of understanding just arises in the group. Smiles and nods and responses of 'yes' emerge as insights shoot across the room. There may be raised voices and even laughter. It appears that the time spent grappling and not-understanding has taken us to an unexpected conclusion. It is as though a kind of group wisdom has occurred. What was not understood now makes sense. The understanding gives rise to interpretation and theorizing. There is a natural next step as people recognize possible applications within their own theses. It appears that learning has occurred. Challenges are not avoided and at the same time the rule of kindness applies. We are not seeking agreement with one another; nor are we seeking disagreement. We are each seeking our 'felt' response to the conversation as we try to continuously stay with the phenomena or concern under discussion.

A conversation about language explores how the complexity of the language of a theoretical system becomes a barrier to the theory. What is the experience of that barrier? And what is it like on either side of that barrier: is it a barrier or is it a protection? We grapple with the nature of language as opening up the nature of understanding and interpretation. Some argue that the language of hermeneutics poses a barrier to its understanding; others speak of the journey into the language as a journey of comprehension. Insight arises about being inside and being outside of your PhD, about the struggle, about finding your purpose.

Playfulness, banter and teasing are part of the culture of the group. In speaking of when and how creativity occurs, we lead to the nature of thoughts taking hold and letting go of one. We argue playfully about the nature of 'being-in' a question and the nature of talking about 'being-in' a question, about how the way into the Circle is through a leap into the Circle – and what does that actually mean? Some take the leap; others prefer the safety of the known. We continue learning what that means.

With seven years behind us, we recognize that the Circle is making a significant difference for candidates. Some candidates appear to need less individualized input from supervisors. Relationships and support dyads and triads are being created. References are exchanged. Papers are being collaborated on. People turn up regularly for the Circle and appear enthusiastic about their research journeys, PhD completions become more frequent.

The above passage has described my experience as immediate perception of the Circle, without interpretation or theorizing, and in keeping with the method of phenomenology where conceptualization follows perception (Merleau-Ponty 1962). The following themes represent a drawing out of some of the central features of the group experience that emerge seamlessly from the description. This pattern is similar to what transpires in the Circle where understanding and interpretation follow experience. It can be noted that these features capture many of the central concepts of phronesis as will be delineated in the next section, which articulates a theoretical overview of phronesis.

Theme: Cultivation of Practice

Participation in the Circle is not sporadic. Through regular attendance and regular reflection on how we participate, it appears that we are actively cultivating our particular way of participating and thereby actively creating the very nature of the Circle. The nature of our participation in the Circle is therefore evolving through both our experience of participation and the reflection on the experience whilst being within the experience of the Circle, regularly. Our practice is thereby being both nurtured and cultivated: a training ground!

Theme: *Playfulness and Humour*

These appear to be intrinsic to the life of the Circle. Whilst our primary task of learning about research and our primary methodology of phenomenology are both complex and engaging activities, a quality of lightness fuels the living nature of the Circle. What is the 'right' amount of lightness? This can only be assessed from within the particular context.

Theme: *Relationship and Dialogue*

The dialogue is inclusive and an essential aspect of the life of the Circle. We try to avoid dominance by a few, frequently inquire of those that have not been vocal, and generally try to ensure that everyone participates without inhibition. The development of the dialogue is in itself a practice that is being cultivated. There have been negative behaviour patterns such as personal criticisms. The nature of the dialogue is frequently attended to through sharing reflections on the dialogue and relationships by the supervisors and, at times, by the candidates themselves.

Theme: *Grappling and Uncertainty*

As supervisors we are suspicious when the conversation is relaxed and logical. We are on the lookout for bringing the conversation back to experience, ensuring that theorizing is arising out of experience. Our understanding is that when we are 'on track' we are theorizing and interpreting. We are operating in the field of 'the known'. When there are levels of discomfort and grappling, it is a sign that we are 'off track'. This is the process that we wish to straddle: the continuous interaction of experience and theory. The 'not-knowing' of the outcome of the conversation takes each person into experience and it is out of the experience of grappling, an all-embracing experience, that insight and learning often appear.

The four themes together

Seen together, the above four themes offer a useful gauge with which to consider the effectiveness of a professional learning group. Without specifying exactly what each feature ought to reveal, they can be applied as a kind of meta-pattern in evaluating a specific group. Each feature can be applied and assessed after a group meeting with questions such as: 'What was the quality of the dialogue today?' A group will develop its own benchmarks according to its needs. The features can provide a reflexive opportunity for the group praxis.

The creation of an intersubjective learning environment operating with hermeneutic principles is best utilized with a group that is wishing to learn or work towards a particular intention. One key ingredient of critical significance is that each member of the group has a self-directed (autotelic) interest in building a particular practice or learning. This implies that such a group would not operate well through coercion. A practice with a hermeneutic phenomenological methodology is therefore best served where each participant is a 'professional' pursuing the understanding of some aspect of professional practice or research.

This inquiry now puts the Circle aside and continues with building an understanding of the nature of phronesis. It begins with Aristotle's description and then a review of how Heidegger and then Gadamer have adopted the notion. Thereafter, I return to the Circle using specific anecdotes that suggest its application within organizational management practices and Higher Education.

Conceptualization of Phronesis: Aristotle and then Heidegger and Gadamer

Phronesis, interpreted as practical wisdom or knowing, arises within Aristotle's (1962) moral and political philosophy. It is distinguished primarily as being an activity of apprehension, the 'how' of knowing, that includes the theoretical (sophia), the practical (phronesis) and the technical (techne) ways of knowing.

Sophia is translated as theoretical wisdom and is seen by Aristotle (1962) as the highest intellectual and philosophical excellence that people are able to reach. For the sake of distinction, sophia can be considered as wisdom, as it is commonly used. Techne can be translated as knowing the techniques that are required to operate well in the world. These are the rules and the skillset that can often be learnt in anticipation of the activity. The difference between techne and phronesis is argued in relation to the debate as to whether medicine involves the knowledge of techne activity or phronesis (Waring 2000). The debate itself will further thoughtfulness and deliberation about the practice of medicine and therefore, in itself, would be considered by Aristotle to be an ethical activity.

Aristotle describes phronesis as an ethical and an intellectual virtue. The essence of the virtues is that they are founded in activity, rather than in knowledge, and arise by being cultivated, exercised and practiced (Ladkin 2010). 'It [phronesis] is an adult trenchancy of insight into practical matters that is cultivated by training and experience' (Aristotle 1962: 1140b: 20). And for this reason, we refer to it as a lived experience.

Central to phronesis is the activity of deliberation about 'living well in general' or about the things which manifest our happiness in 'living well as a whole'. Thus the sense of 'doing well' is an essential concern of phronesis. Aristotle describes it thus: phronesis is a 'state grasping the truth, involving reason, and concerned with action about human goods' (1962: 1140b5). It implies further that the appreciation of 'doing well' is not according to externally created rules but rather the answers arise from within the context of the deliberating on what 'doing well' means. Hence community becomes integral in the development of phronesis.

Phronesis, as a way of knowing, necessarily involves action and relationality, dialogue and deliberation (Ladkin 2010). Whether an action is phronetic depends on whether the person acts knowingly, chooses the act for its own sake and acts from a firm and unshakeable disposition. The example given by Aristotle (1962) is that the knowledge of the theory of moral philosophy will not result in moral behaviour. Whilst phronesis is concerned with universals, it must also recognize the particulars; it is practical, and practice is concerned with particulars. Apprehension, therefore, arises out of the deliberate (for its own sake) engagement in the particulars of the practice. The action of the Circle is continuously a deliberation about research whilst at the same time, being within and doing research.

The activity or actioning of phronesis is praxis. Praxis is guided by the purpose (intentionality) of phronesis. A person's action is considered to be praxis if they are acting for the sake of acting rightly within the particular circumstances; that is they are not following rules or acting for the purpose of a particular or external outcome (Kemmis 2011).

Heidegger's Transformation

For Heidegger the practical philosophy of Aristotle is a guiding thread in his analysis of existence (1962; 1995) according to which facticity names our unique mode of being-in-the-world. Through his 'existential analytic', Heidegger recognizes that 'Aristotelian phenomenology' suggests three fundamental movements of life – poiesis, praxis and theoria – and that these have three corresponding dispositions: techne, phronesis and sophia. Heidegger considers these as modalities of being inherent in the structure of 'Dasein' as being-in-the-world that is situated within the context of concern and care. According to Heidegger, phronesis in Aristotle's work discloses the right and proper way to be 'Dasein'. This means that Heidegger sees phronesis as a mode of comportment in and towards the world, a way of orienting oneself and thus of caring-seeing-knowing and enabling a particular way of being concerned. Whilst techne is a way of being concerned with things and principles of production and theoria a way of being concerned with eternal principles, phronesis is a way of being concerned with one's life as action in relation to the lives of others and to all particular circumstances and this is the scope of praxis (Smith 2003). Thus phronesis is a disposition or habit, which reveals the being of the action, whilst its deliberation is the mode of bringing about the disclosive nature of that action. In other words, deliberation is the way in which the phronetic nature of Dasein's insight is made manifest.

Weidenfeld (2011) argues that a number of Heidegger's meaningful activities are considered equivalent to Aristotle's phronesis. A particular situation is a primary determinant for phronesis. The 'in the practice' learning of practice is the preparation needed for doing the right thing in the appropriate moment and practice is learnt in the place that the practice happens. The concerns of for-the-sake-of-which (worumwillen) are guided by circumspection (Umsicht). Heidegger himself translates phronesis as Umsicht and 'for-the-sake-of-which' is Dasein itself. Umsicht points to the capacity for making sense of practical situations that thereby become a phenomenological account of phronesis. 'Whenever we have something to contribute or perform, circumspection gives us the route for proceeding with it, the means of carrying it out, the right opportunity, the appropriate moment' (Heidegger 1962: 216).

An example is that of the teacher who learns what is needed to be an effective teacher only in the classroom in front of students (situatedness). Techne alone cannot create excellence in a teacher, and the idea of poor teaching does not eventuate because of poor technical skills alone. The discerning of what is required to be excellent and the embedding of those skills is through circumspection, which occurs through the experience of teaching. The knowledge does not arise in detached reflection, rather it is revealed through the experience and doing of teaching as a phronetic praxis.

Heidegger's adoption of Aristotle's phronesis is broadened rather brilliantly by a further level of conceptualization. Because it is the person him or herself who is ultimately the judge or referral point about the relative benefit of the knowing how to act, Heidegger includes conscience (Gewissen) as further implicated in phronesis. In wishing to act well, one is concerned about one's own 'be-ing' rather than another's assessment of acting well. Weidenfeld (2011) suggests that conscience is an extreme form of circumspection and is tied to the moment of vision. This is the moment that recognizes the unique features of the actual situation. Examples of this include humour where a situation shows up as funny; moments of insight or vision arise because of the 'resolute' individual that discloses them as such. Thus humour only makes sense in relation to the particular situation. Further, conscience respects the norms and behaviours that are particular to that situation. Phronesis discloses the concrete ways of being within a particular situation and it is this disclosure that gives rise to self-understanding. Within the hermeneutic dialogue process, disclosure arises through the reflection of 'being with the question'. Overall, Heidegger shows how phronesis discloses the concrete possibilities of being-in a situation, as the starting point of meaningful action, processed with resolution, whilst facing the contingencies of life.

The Transition to Gadamer

In Gadamerian hermeneutics, phronesis is connected to practice whereby reflexive understanding itself is understood as a way of being through having ontological significance, and through being situated in a hermeneutic context. Phronesis is a kind of knowing that is conceptualized as an experience with both historical and dialectic meaning and, as such, is more than a perceptual act of knowing. Such an act of knowing is like an encounter or an event (Palmer 1969).

Gadamer disagrees with Hegel's concept of experience whereby awareness is 'restructured' and a new object of knowledge is generated or born out of it (Palmer 1969). Rather, Gadamer suggests that experience fulfils itself through the openness to experience (Gadamer 1984: 320): 'what is properly gained from all experience then, is to know what is'. But 'what is', here, is not this or that thing, but 'what cannot be done away with' – that which cannot be done away with includes *tradition* where tradition has the same meaning in experience as *text* has in relation to hermeneutics. We necessarily belong to a tradition; which exists before we do. We may or may not be conscious of it, but we always already find ourselves within a tradition which influences and shapes our existence and thinking. Historicality thereby has significance, as historical thinking has to account for its own history. Similarly our thinking needs to take account of the traditions in which we find ourselves. Finding out about such a matter is a continuous process and as Gadamer says, we are always 'on the way' to such self-knowledge. In relation to the dialectic aspect of phronesis, Gadamer describes the concept of horizon as all that can be seen (or known) from a particular position or vantage point. Horizons are thereby both limited and finite and at the same time fluid and changing.

Gadamer (1977) describes phronesis as the action of opening oneself to the truth that speaks through tradition. Phronesis therefore serves as a model for hermeneutics as it is a mode of uncovering truth in action. Moreover the way towards knowledge and the understanding of a horizon is a dialectical movement with another. Whilst each person is grounded in their own situation, each horizon is enlarged and enriched through a fusion of horizons between the speaker and listeners. It is through this dialogue that we gain knowledge of ourselves. As Sandy (2011: 275) suggests, 'Gadamer's treatment of phronesis emphasizes the openness of conversation, ongoing participation that may lead to friendship, and processes for deliberating on the common good'. Accordingly, he focuses largely on the communicative and the creative dimensions of practical wisdom.

Dialogue, Disruption and the Intersubjective Space

A senior manager in a large telecommunications organization embarked on his PhD preoccupied by the word 'stupid'. His sense of frustration was the extent of 'stupid' decisions taken in his workplace including 'stupid' actions of some managers, the waste of money and time, and general poor communication, and, of course, the frustration of his inability to change the culture. As a group, we listened carefully to the candidate's experience. Focusing on the word 'stupid', we noticed the emotions that were arising and through the conversation built an understanding of how 'stupid' as a phenomenon manifests. In the process, we uncovered some powerful insights into the nature of being a manager, into the nature of the student himself and into the nature of the workplace.

Robert Romanyshyn, author of *The Wounded Researcher* (2007), names the experience of disruption that may lead to undertaking a PhD, a kind of wounding. He suggests that the linking with vulnerability actually cements the candidate to their topic. Romanyshyn describes this as a shift from the tough-minded neutral observer to the vulnerable observer. Through the engagement in the Circle with his experience (of 'stupid'), the candidate faced his historicality: the traditions that he emerges out of, his work life conventions or expectations, personal ethics, and the context of the business of telecommunications companies. His horizon became known to himself and to the others. The dialectic of conversation meant that his horizon fused with others through being heard and understood. The historical and the dialectic aspects of the experience led to a transformation of the phenomenon and his management practice began to be understood in relation to anomalies and paradoxes. Furthermore, 'anomaly' is not for him a detached but an embodied concept that describes a wide range of work experiences. The insights that have arisen and the action that has been adopted would have been unlikely without the dialectic with his actual experience. This is consistent with the Heideggerian proposition that to question is to be in question and thus the research questions emerge out of the way he is in question, in the being-in of his professional practice.

When meaning arises out of intersubjective communication that is orientated towards mutual understanding, it corroborates Habermas's (1971) term, 'intersubjective co-creativity'. Intersubjective agreement is the foundation of consensual scientific knowledge established between communicating individuals. This becomes like a mutual beholding where the experience of consciousness arises as a felt experience as a result of the encounter. Further it is through this network of linguistically mediated interactions that self-knowledge emerges (Bernstein 1988).

Gadamer (1998) speaks of how a hermeneutic approach embraces perspective as the only way through which understanding is made possible. The concrete instance provides the access to understanding (the part is used to access the whole or vice versa). A phenomenon such as 'stupid' would be disavowed in most academic environments. However its expression provided a unique horizon for the candidate and the group. The continued deliberation on the phenomenon has given rise to new insight and action. The intersubjective environment provided the creative forum for the phenomenon to be described, understood and interpreted.

Management and Professional Practice

Whilst some candidates will pursue the PhD for professional promotion, especially an academic career, the majority of our candidates decide to do a PhD because of a sense of disruption, discomfort or curiosity within their professional lives as consultants or managers. They are driven by their particular experience of their practices, bringing a powerful intention of caring to their work and they therefore already have a kind of embodied knowledge that is more than they can tell or speak of. This is the source of their intentionality that appears to provide the grist for their entire thesis. Moreover it is within their praxis as professionals in the world of management that phronesis is sought. Due to space constrictions, I offer one anecdote that shows a significant shift in judgement with regard to a fundamental principle of professional practice.

> He has been an independent project manager in information technology for over 20 years. He was troubled by the inhumane expectations that arise within a scientific approach to project management where every project is considered a failure. Through his research, which included the reflection on project management as a phenomenon from within project management, he has taken a 'hermeneutic turn' and reconfigured his ways of thinking about project management. He recently headed and completed a $15 million project for a major airline in record time (nine months) and maintained the best possible relationships within the work environment. The client was satisfied with the outcomes. He ran the entire project by using a hermeneutic rather than a positivist approach to project management. He describes how the first third of the project time was building relationships and clarifying the goals and objectives for the project. Furthermore, only when every stakeholder had reached agreement on the simple two-page document outlining the goals, did the application begin.

This candidate has integrated a hermeneutic approach to his professional practice, and recognized the significance of careful listening and connection in order to operationalize a project effectively. He has broken from traditional practices and taken action that reflects his subtle or tacit knowledge of his profession.

Research: Embodied Knowing and Understanding

> By wisdom – I mean an often ineffable knowing born of direct experience, a kind of intuitive pragmatism that works to the extent that it takes account of the whole. It is inclusive and invariably involves empathy and compassion
>
> (de Quincey 2005: 36)

A senior army officer is doing his PhD on leadership. He remembers the pictures of past war heroes that his father used to show him as a child and shows these same photos to the group. Then he speaks with some pain of his relationship with his father. He thereby situates and understands his passion and his pain that surround the phenomenon of leadership for him.

Through the engagement with his historicality, this candidate has arrived at a point of embodied knowing about leadership and his research that shapes his relationship with the phenomenon of leadership. The presence of the group assisted this candidate to connect with the moment of vision whereby the features of that situation could be clearly recognized. For Gadamer, the desire to seek understanding is also the desire to be understood by another. Genuinely speaking one's mind is not simply about explication but rather encompasses the idea of relationship: of involvement with someone. This process of developing a point of view is a process of developing the not-yet-fully-understood aspects of your subject more clearly into focus. 'To reach an understanding with one's partner in a dialogue is not merely a matter of total self-expression and the successful assertion of one's point of view, but a transformation into a communion, in which we do not remain who we were' (Gadamer 1998: 341).

It is interesting to notice that the word 'conscientia' means 'knowing with' others (de Quincey 2005). Thus, originally the word 'consciousness' implied a dialogic process. To be conscious means that two or more people are privy to the process of insight emergence. Gadamer illuminates his clear dismissal of knowledge as merely conceptual data. The act of knowing is closer to the action of perception. 'There is no such thing as a method of learning to ask questions; of learning to see what needs to be questioned' (Gadamer 1998: 329). He says thinking gives rise to questioning and that all this transpires in the art of conducting real conversation. In this situation, knowing becomes a happening; it is an experience, a kind of real life understanding that arises in the moment which we may even call wisdom (ibid.).

Management author Nonaka (2004) writes about organizational knowledge and its creation. Consistent with Gadamer (1998), he suggests that creative dialogues give rise to tacit knowledge and that this occurs through images (experience/perceptions) being shared through metaphorical processes and merging perspectives. He argues that authentic knowledge comes about through a spiralling movement between the explicit and the tacit dimensions of knowledge. Such knowledge is enriched and enlarged for individuals and organizations and gives rise to building a 'truly humanistic knowledge society' (Nonaka 2004: 197). In his book *Radical Knowing*, de Quincey (2005: 58) says: 'Intention is an expression of who we are into the world – it is sourced in the self and then directed outward.' The human experience is central in the act of knowing, the awareness of one's individual horizons and the fusion with others.

Through Being-in the Hermeneutic Circle

The following are candidates' comments as a quick response to the question of what they appreciate about their experience of the Circle:

> The positive and non-competitive environment; everything becomes relevant; embracing alternative ways of thinking; supporting individual ways of thinking and individual voices; deepening understanding of what it means to do research; the opportunity of listening and being listened to; the opportunity to practice silence, respect and spiritual ideas; the opportunity to share your stories – successes and celebrations; it offers a real emotional climate; I was doing someone else's thesis, now I'm doing my own.

When a group meets regularly there is the potential for each person to become a conduit for others' learning and knowing and thus an intersubjective space of knowing arises. Most of the candidates' professional lives and work, their praxis, has been significantly affected through their engagement with the Circle. Through the action of the candidate coming to 'know' his or her subject through the practice of being-in question with others, through the challenge of the dialogue, through the deliberations, their intentions achieve authority (authorship) and validation. The researcher therefore necessarily becomes implicated in any research conducted. And this suggests a question about what we really mean by Higher Education.

Higher Education: Towards a 'Gentle Empiricism'

Arthur Zajonc (in Palmer and Zajonc 2010), scientist and educator, expresses the goals of the educational process through situating education within the paradigm of the new sciences. Heisenberg's uncertainty principle, dating back to the 1920s, has long ago specified that the goal of research is no longer about nature itself, but rather about the researcher's investigation of nature. With the world not independent from the knower, the conscious human being is necessarily part of any findings and knowledge becomes more of an event than an object, with human experience at the forefront of what is found. Gadamer would surely agree that the real work of researching is to extend experience and to use reason and reflection to find the possible interrelationships of experience. Goethe (in Bortoft 1996: 223) suggests that 'every object well contemplated opens a new organ of perception in us'. The capacity to approach the object of our attention, the phenomenon at hand, without distorting it or changing it requires gentleness, a kind of 'gentle empiricism' (zarte Empirie).

The greatest impediment to understanding a thing or phenomenon comes from the need to explain it in terms of something else. Explanation results in each thing becoming an instance or example that can analytically be seen to belong to a group, perhaps a bit more or less like that group. Understanding a phenomenon is a way of grasping it as a whole. Also Wittgenstein (in Bortoft 1996) describes understanding as the seeing of the connections intrinsic to the phenomenon. He appreciates this kind of seeing as an imaginative capacity, operating beyond the senses, and demanding a particular level of engagement in the researcher to be receptive to the phenomenon in its wholeness. It is as though this imaginative sense fuels the ongoing inquiry creating what Palmer and Zajonc (2010: 94) refer to as a 'contemplative inquiry'.

In discussing the aspirations of education, Kemmis (2011) longs for the goals that the ancients in Aristotle's time had of bringing people to learn wisdom so that the world would be worth living in. Education was not geared towards the skills of a field of expertise. He suggests that education is best suited towards giving people the particular kinds of experiences that will lead them to wisdom. Moreover practice-based approaches are best suited to this. Correspondingly, the Circle provides such a practice-based education and experience of praxis within research and an academic institution! Bernstein (1988) suggests that Gadamer's interpretation of Aristotle's text is an exemplar of hermeneutical understanding and that Aristotle's analysis of phronesis serves as a model for hermeneutics; it is a mode of uncovering truth in action. As a hermeneutical understanding is itself a form of practical reasoning and practical knowledge it is a form of phronesis (Bernstein 1988)!

In general consideration of the academic environment, there is little to prepare candidates for their actual experience of PhD research. It is a pathway that causes many candidates to stumble and fail. The hermeneutic dialectic process provides a kind of gentle empiricism where the learning is engaging and the candidate's needs for a satisfying Higher Education experience are sated. Over the years, my observation is that the mood of the group has become both lighter and also more considered; we judge less, respond slower and offer greater discernment. A new kind of respect appears to be developing: the respect for difference. In a letter to Bernstein (1988: 264), Gadamer comments on the non-exceptionality of conflict: 'Phronesis is always the process of distinguishing and choosing what one considers to be right.' Perhaps as a group, in a Higher Education environment, incorporating a 'gentle empiricism', we are also learning judgement!

In Conclusion

The appropriate Aristotelian dialectic on this case study could be: is the Circle good for the practice of research? Is the Circle good for the practice of Higher Education? And is the Circle good for the practice of management? In response, Gadamer (1998: 319) may reply: 'the dialectic of experience has its own fulfilment not in definitive knowledge, but in that openness to experience that is encouraged by experience itself'. That none of the participants have dropped out of their PhDs or the Circle and that their enthusiasm for their research seems to increase are pointers to a conclusion that the experience of the Circle is itself satisfying. There is an active interest in continuing the conversation.

Green (2009) suggests that the case study as a way of documenting professional practice could usefully be brought back into our attention as researchers and as practitioners. And this is not simply to rewrite more of the same case studies, but rather to reconsider its usage in what he calls 'a qualitative, practice-theoretical mode of meta-analysis' (Green 2009: 15). With other authors such as Polkinghorne (2007) and Flyvberg (2004), I believe that the use of case study to inquire into practice provides an invaluable resource. This chapter has attempted to achieve a richly descriptive weaving of anecdote and narrative towards capturing a sense of the practice of the Circle. At the same time, using the lens of phronesis has offered layers of observation, understanding, interpretation and judgement to the analysis that has hopefully elevated the case and brought an insightful engagement.

Through the writing up of this case study, another question that begs consideration is the potential generalizability of the practice of a hermeneutic phenomenological dialectic approach within management practice and within academic environments. Whilst some consideration has been given to this topic throughout the chapter, it is useful to reiterate some of the preconditions. This may include: the topic is personally meaningful to all participants (intentionality); that each person participate without coercion (autotelic); and that participants are prepared for a disciplined inquiry where purpose and direction can be mutually created (intersubjectivity). One question that applies the use of a professional learning group working with cases is: With the goal of discovering ways of thinking that did not previously exist, could it be that a professional learning group could surpass the capacity of a single manager to find creative solutions to arising issues?

Further, before beginning this work, potential members of the group would best be educated and prepared for the nature of this practice, as each person plays a vital role in its creation; actually each person takes up a leadership role. Given that the practitioner dialogue described has a clear developmental or formative aspect for the individuals, could a learning group of the nature of 'the Circle' be used to enhance or stimulate leadership capacity or further develop leadership for managers?

Given that learning is significant to management as it is in educational institutions, a question that begs further research is: How can phronesis and the Circle be applied as a goal towards developing thoughtfulness and judgement and gearing our learning towards the 'good', as a goal for the society, the environment and the self?

References

Aristotle, 1962, *Nicomachean Ethics*, translated with introduction and notes by Martin Oswald, Indianapolis: The Bobbs-Merrill Company.

Bernstein, R J, 1988, *Beyond Objectivism and Relativism: Science, Hermeneutics, and Praxis*, Philadelphia: University of Pennsylvania Press.

Bohm, D, 1990, *On Dialogue*, Ojai: David Bohm Seminars.

Bortoft, H, 1996, *The Wholeness of Nature: Goethe's Way of Science*, Edinburgh: Floris Books.

Coulter, D and Wiens, J R, 2002, Educational judgment: linking the actor and the spectator, *Educational Researcher*, 31(4), 15–25.

de Quincey, C, 2005, *Radical Knowing: Understanding Consciousness through Relationship*, Rochester: Park Street Press.

Flyvbjerg, B, 2002, One researcher's praxis story, *Journal of Planning Education and Research*, 21(4), 353–66.

Flyvbjerg, B, 2004, Phronetic planning research: theoretical and methodological reflections, *Planning Theory & Practice*, 5(3), 283–306.

Gadamer, H G, 1977, *Philosophical Hermeneutics*, translated and edited by D E Linge, Berkeley: University of California Press.

Gadamer, H G, 1984, *Truth and Method*, New York: The Crossroad Publishing Company.

Green, B, 2009, Introduction: understanding and researching professional practice, in *Understanding and Researching Professional Practice*, edited by B Green, Rotterdam: Sense Publishers, 1–18.

Habermas, J, 1971, *Knowledge and Human Interests*, translated by Jeremy Shapiro, Boston: Beacon Press.

Heidegger, M, 1962, *Being and Time*, Oxford: Blackwell.

Heidegger, M, 1995, *Aristotle's Metaphysics*, Bloomington: Indiana University Press.

Higgs, J, Paterson, M and Kinsella, E A, 2012, Hermeneutic inquiry: interpretation and understanding in research practice, *Contemporary Psychotherapy*, 4(1) [Online], Available at: http://contemporarypsychotherapy.org/vol-4-no-1-spring-2012/hermeneutic-inquiry/ [accessed: 29 July 2012].

Jankelson, Claire, 2013, *Phronesis in Action: A Case Study Approach to a Professional Learning Group in A Handbook of Practical Wisdom*, edited by W Kupers and D J Pauleen, England: Gower, 47–63.

Kemmis, S, 2011, Pedagogy, praxis and practice-based higher education, in *Practice-Based Education*, edited by J Higgs, R Barnett and S Billet, Rotterdam: Sense, 1–17.

Ladkin, D, 2010, Book Review on Olav Eikeland, The Ways of Aristotle: Aristotelian Phronesis, Aristotelian Philosophy of Dialogue, and Action Research, *Action Research*, 8(4), 444–8.

Merleau-Ponty, M, 1962, *Phenomenology of Perception*, London: Routledge; Humanities Press.

Nonaka, I, 2004, A dynamic theory of organizational knowledge creation, in *How Organizations Learn*, edited by K Starkey, S Tempest and A Mckinlay, London: Thomson, 165–201.

Palmer, P and Zajonc, A, 2010, *The Heart of Higher Education*, San Francisco: Jossey-Bass.

Palmer, R E, 1969, *Hermeneutics*, Evanston: Northwestern University Press.

Polkinghorne, D E, 2007, Language and meaning: data collection in qualitative research, *Qualitative Inquiry*, 13(4), 471–86.

Romanyshyn, R, 2007, *The Wounded Researcher*, New Orleans: Spring Journal Books.

Sandy, M, 2011, Practical beauty and the legacy of pragmatism: generating theory for community-engaged scholarship, *Interchange*, 42(3), 261–85.

Smith, D L, 2003, Intensifying phronesis: Heidegger, Aristotle, and rhetorical culture, *Philosophy and Rhetoric*, 36(1), 77–102.

Waring, D, 2000, Why the practice of medicine is not a phronetic activity, *Theoretical Medicine and Bioethics*, 21(2), 139–51.

Weidenfeld, M C, 2011, Heidegger's appropriation of Aristotle: phronesis, con-science, and seeing through the one, *European Journal of Political Theory*, 10(2), 254–76.

Chapter 2

Stuck between Management Theory and a Hard Place

The Lived Experience of Managing in the Space between Senior Management and the Real World

Darcy Duggan

Human beings like things to make sense. We seek to come to an under-standing of our world with our fellow humans through shared language and practices. This shared understanding forms a common ground upon which we can build a meaningful world together and a place for ourselves within that world.

This chapter originates from my own attempts to make sense of the world, and especially from experiences I have had where those attempts have failed miserably. Many of these experiences have occurred in the workplace. I have detailed a number of them in two personal accounts which appear in the following pages. At the centre of my failed attempts to make sense of my workplace is the relationship between the expected and the unexpected.

Hans-Georg Gadamer's hermeneutics revolves around experiences of familiarity and strangeness. Whether we are seeking to understand a written text or an experience within our socially constructed world, we bring with us a set of expectations and preconceptions that lead us to anticipate meaning. However Gadamer says we will only be able to come to a true understanding of the meaning of a text or social interaction by maintaining an orientation of openness to what it has to say to us. By remaining open we will notice ele-ments that are both familiar to us, as well as strange. Understanding occurs in this space between familiarity and strangeness. Gadamer says, 'The true locus of hermeneutics is this in-between' (Gadamer 2013, p. 306).

I attempt to understand and describe the experience of managing in the space between familiarity and strangeness at work. Specifically, what being at work is like when what I am being told to do doesn't make sense, but I find myself doing it anyway. My experience of this phenomenon in the workplace is captured by Thomas Kuhn's notion of anomaly (Kuhn 1996).

This chapter investigates an approach to management practice that can be applied to such situations to bring about a new set of shared practices. This approach comes from the work of Charles Spinosa, Fernando Flores and Hubert Dreyfus and is based on the hermeneutic phenomenology of Martin

Heidegger. Central to this approach is the experience of disharmony and of anomaly; concepts Spinosa et al. relate to the work of Thomas Kuhn.

Phenomenological questions arise as we go about our business in the world These types of questions bring to front of mind aspects of our understanding that were previously taken for granted and unexamined. For Gadamer, phenomenological questioning begins with an experience of an object that produces something other than what we expected to see.

> We have experiences when we are shocked by things that do not accord with our expectations. . . . A question presses itself in on us; we can no longer avoid it and persist in our accustomed opinion.
>
> (Gadamer 2013, p. 375)

In order to explain something of the context from which my questions about the meaning of management emerged, I begin with an account of my own experience of anomaly as a new manager in a large Australian corporation.

In the second section I define the term anomaly based on the work of Thomas Kuhn, before presenting three attempts from academia to describe and learn from the experience of anomaly. In the first of these Tony Watson gives an ethnographic account of management practices at a large telecommunications company. In the second Karl Weick explains how academics might gain valuable insights from managers working in the midst of anomaly which could help them build better theories of management practice. Finally, Fernando Flores demonstrates how management practice can be transformed by remaining sensitive to anomaly as it shows up for him while he goes about his business. He does this by using an example from his own experience as a manager. Flores' experience is taken up by Spinosa et al. in their discussion of how anomaly can be used to reconfigure shared practices in society.

In the next section I propose an adaption of Spinosa et al.'s approach to working with anomaly that can be applied to business management practice. This approach provides management practitioners with an opportunity to identify and reflect on aspects of our shared management practices that are normally in the background, hidden from view. I will use an account from my workplace experience to demonstrate how, by remaining sensitive to the anomaly as it presents itself in the midst of our ongoing practice, management practitioners can experiment with new ways of practising which resolve rather than ignore the anomaly.

My Experience of Anomaly as a New Manager

For ten years I worked for a large Australian utility company in technical and management roles in the area of service delivery. As a technician, I often shared a joke with my colleagues about management decisions we considered 'stupid'. Cost saving measures such as cutting overtime, limiting work related travel or putting off the purchase of essential test equipment saved money in the short term, but threatened long term profitability in fairly predictable ways. These measures slowed down the rate at which we delivered services and delayed the turn-on of revenue. Our Sales teams complained that we were hurting the customers and making it extremely hard for them to secure repeat business.

I eventually became a manager of a service delivery team within the Operations division. My job was to ensure that 90 per cent of services were delivered on-time. The performance of all service delivery teams was monitored daily. Every Monday began with management meetings about the performance from the previous week. If a service was not delivered on-time we had to know why. We were constantly hunting for 'root causes' and 'systemic issues'. It was believed that this type of analysis would lead to continuous improvement of our processes and, by default, improved performance.

All of the service delivery teams achieved, or bettered, their on-time performance target most weeks. Despite this, the Sales teams consistently complained that the customers were not happy with our service delivery. They said we were regularly moving out customer delivery dates to make our performance look better than it really was, and that we were regularly taking much longer than promised to deliver a service. The Sales teams' claims were given credence by the company's customer feedback reports where customers regularly gave the service delivery teams a score of around 65 per cent for on-time delivery.

Staff in the service delivery teams were allowed to move delivery dates if the customer requested the change or if they were not ready for us to install the service on the date they had originally requested. However, over time, a number of spurious practices had developed to justify the revision of delivery dates. This included calling customers with little or no notice to request site access to connect a service, often late on the day the service was due. This often resulted in the customer requesting a later date. Alternately, in these situations the customer was often not contactable. Both these scenarios allowed the service delivery people to revise the delivery date and attribute it to a 'customer delay'.

I would like to be able to say that I was able to stop my team from moving out delivery dates without good cause. I attempted to do this in the early days of my management, and my team was happy to comply. They didn't actually like the practices they'd adopted. Some of the old hands quietly told me 'all the new managers have a go at doing this, but within a month things go back to normal'. The old timers were right. After a few weeks the team's performance had steadily dropped to as low as 60 per cent. The pressure to get the on-time performance to back up over 90 per cent was intense.

When I started in management I was determined that I would not be the author of 'stupid' management decisions. Now I felt I was failing as a manager. I was trying to succeed at the task I had been given but I felt the accepted ways of doing things in my organisation were preventing this. When I tried to challenge these practices (with my manager and with my peers) I got nowhere. After a short while my colleagues began referring to my 'soap box' whenever I raised these matters. I stopped rocking the boat for fear of being thrown overboard. I focused on getting the numbers back up and didn't scrutinise the behaviour around delivery date changes too heavily. Within my team we all adopted an unspoken 'don't ask, don't tell' policy. The performance numbers came back up to 90 per cent. My manager was happy and there were long periods of time where I was happy with my team's performance and with the quality of my work. My team could really pull out the stops and get a great result for a customer when we had to.

However the complaints from the various Sales teams continued and eventually the director of the Operations division agreed to conduct monthly audits on the validity of delivery date changes. I was asked to oversee these audits. Managers from each service delivery team would randomly select a number of services whose delivery dates had been moved to a later date during the previous month. I would receive a report detailing whether these moves were in accordance with approved guidelines. Often the errors could be explained away as a misunderstanding between the technicians and administrative people whose job it was to change the delivery dates. I would use this information to prepare a report for the senior managers in Sales. The audits brought an end to our more spurious practices around date changes and succeeded in hosing down overt criticism from Sales about our management of delivery dates. Apart from that, things pretty much stayed the same. Day to day murmurings from the Sales teams continued, customer satisfaction levels stayed low and the on-time performance numbers stayed high.

I continued to oversee the audits which found no systemic issue around date changes. But I was still uncomfortable with our behaviour in this area. I was the one defending our practices and our performance figures, but secretly I was deeply suspicious of both. My colleagues did not disagree with my suspicions, but saw these practices as unavoidable. For some, it was simply a sign of the tension inherent in trying to keep customers, staff and shareholders all happy at the same time.

Whatever justification was used, the message was that this was not a problem we needed to fix. It was just something 'we had to live with'. For me, 'living with' became synonymous with 'remaining silent'. I didn't feel able to have an authentic, no holds barred conversation about what was broken in our way of working. And if this way of managing wasn't allowed, I didn't really know how to act anymore.

In my last year as a manager, I was awarded the company's highest performance rating. That year I turned down a promotion and left the company. In the end it didn't matter to me that the reports looked good. I knew I wasn't performing.

After leaving the company I spent 18 months out of the workforce building a house before deciding that I would like to return to management work. I felt that I needed some training to enable me to do a better job of it this time around. I enrolled in a Master of Management degree.

A Theoretical Perspective on the Experience of Anomaly at Work

The story I have just recounted centres on my experience of a phenomenon that can be labelled 'anomaly'. This term derives from the work of Thomas Kuhn (1996) that is outlined in this section. Problems arose for me when my encounter with management and with managing did not accord with my existing understanding of what management was. Over time I found I was unable to reconcile my pre-understanding and my experience. This conflict escalated to the point where it derailed my practice. I had to admit to myself, not only that I was no longer able to manage, but that I no longer knew what management was.

The ability of anomaly to derail and ultimately transform the practice of science is the focus of Kuhn's work. Many academics have investigated the impact of similar phenomena on the practice of business management. A variety of terms are used, namely 'interruptions' (Weick 2003), 'unready-to-hand moments' (Martin Heidegger in Weick 2003), 'disharmonious practices' (Flores 2000), 'disharmonies' (Spinosa et al. 1997) and 'disorienting dilemmas' (Segal 1999). In this section I will review a number of theoretical approaches to describing and dealing with anomaly in the workplace. I conclude with my own definition of anomaly and how I think it should be dealt with by management practitioners.

A Definition of Anomaly Based on the Work of Thomas Kuhn

Kuhn defines normal science as 'research firmly based upon one or more past scientific achievements that some particular scientific community acknowledges for a time as supplying the foundation for its further practice' (1996, p. 10). These achievements, expounded since the early nineteenth century in text books and in earlier times in classics such as Aristotle's *Physica*, Ptolemy's *Almagest*, Newton's *Principia* and *Opticks*, Franklin's *Electricity*, Lavoisier's *Chemistry* and Lyell's *Geology*, defined for future scientists what constituted a legitimate problem and method for future research (Kuhn 1996, p. 10).

Two essential characteristics of these achievements enabled them to have this influence according to Kuhn. The achievement was seen and widely accepted as an unprecedented leap forwards and it drew a large number of scientists away from competing lines of inquiry. The achievement also opened up a large number of new lines of inquiry for the newly energised researchers to pursue. Kuhn calls scientific achievements that share these two characteristics 'paradigms' (1996, p. 10).

Kuhn further explains that the emergence of a paradigm results in the eventual collapse of competing schools of thought. This is due in part to the conversion of scientists to the paradigm and also to the 'reading out' of those who remain true to the remaining schools, as adherents to the new paradigm simply ignore their work. This has distinct advantages. Kuhn claims that the end of interschool debate eliminates the need for scientists to constantly reiterate fundamentals and reduces the research focus to a select group of phenomena (1996, p. 10).

Because an accepted paradigm affords its researchers an accepted set of first principles, work can start immediately on increasingly subtle and eso-teric problems. Research under these conditions is Kuhn's 'normal science' and success, measured in terms of progress, is more or less a given: 'In short, it is only during periods of normal science that progress seems both obvious and assured' (1996, pp. 163–64).

Kuhn demonstrates the power of anomaly to disrupt the practice of science. It does this by calling into question the paradigm upon which that practice is based. First the scientist becomes aware from his/her research results that something is amiss. It is against the background of taken-for-granted assump-tions inherent in the scientist's paradigm that the new phenomenon appears anomalous. In other words, there is nothing essentially odd, or anomalous about the phenomenon itself. It simply appears odd when the scientist tries to interpret it against what s/he thinks s/he already knows. It is the interac-tion between the phenomenon as it appears to the scientist, and the paradigm under which s/he operates, which gives birth to the anomaly.

A key aspect of the experience of anomaly as Kuhn describes it, is that the scientist begins his/her research concerned about one thing and ends up concerned about one or more fundamental aspects of his/her practice. S/he goes in knowing what s/he knows and having firm expectations about what s/he will learn about the particular problem under investigation. But after discovering the anomaly, the theoretical foundation from which s/he was asking his/her original question becomes for him/her an object of concern. At this point the tables are turned. Instead of the paradigm providing the schema from which the phenomenon under investigation is interpreted, the anomalous phenomenon becomes central to the process of questioning the assumptions of the paradigm.

As we have seen, 'normal science' is, according to Kuhn, paradigm based science. But when the paradigm is in crisis, scientists are forced to do science without a stable paradigm, the very thing that, up to that point, has made science possible. So what does it mean to be a scientist when your paradigm begins to crumble beneath you? Kuhn describes it as 'living in world out of joint' (1996, p. 79). Albert Einstein described the experience like this: 'It was as if the ground had been pulled out from under one, with no firm foundation to be seen anywhere, upon which one could have built' (Kuhn 1996, p. 83) Wolfgang Pauli in a letter to a friend about the crisis in quantum mechanics prior to 1925, lamented: 'At the moment physics is again terribly confused. In any case, it is too difficult for me, and I wish I had been a movie comedian or something of the sort and had never heard of physics' (Kuhn 1996, p. 84).

During periods of crisis the once strict controls of the paradigm begin to loosen. Resolving the anomaly becomes the central focus of more and more of the community's best scientists. As the anomaly continues to resist attempts to resolve it, different scientists begin to investigate the phenomenon via different articulations of the paradigm. At this point the paradigm still exists although there is no longer a general agreement on its fundamental nature. Kuhn calls this mode of practice 'extraordinary science'. It is characterised by 'the proliferation of competing articulations, the willingness to try anything, the expression of explicit discontent, the recourse to philosophy and . . . debate over fundamentals' (1996, p. 91).

Amidst all of this turmoil there are a number of scientists who, according to Kuhn, remain faithful to the old paradigm. Kuhn believes that this resistance cannot be explained away as simple stubbornness. Instead it is a reflection of the nature of scientific research. These scientists' careers have been well served by the assumption that their paradigm is capable of resolving all the scientific problems of their field of research. Kuhn argues that it is this level of confidence that makes normal science possible. It is also for this reason that complete conversion to the new paradigm is linked with generational change. 'Conversions will occur a few at a time until, after the last holdouts have died, the whole profession will again be practising under a single, but now a different, paradigm' (Kuhn 1996, p. 152).

Scientists operating under this new paradigm now see the world in a new way. It is only at this point that the new phenomenon becomes scientific fact. It is no longer the source of anomalous results. Instead it provides fundamental, taken-for-granted assumptions for the new paradigm. The anomaly has become the new normal.

The phenomenon of anomaly is not unique to the field of scientific research. A number of academics have written about the impact of anomaly on management practice. I will now detail three examples of this work.

Tony Watson: An Ethnographic Perspective on Anomaly in the Workplace

The work of Tony Watson (1994) provides an example of an academic research project that could produce opportunities to learn from anomalous experiences in the workplace. Watson, a professor of organisational and managerial behaviour at Nottingham Business School, believes there is a problematic divide between management academics and management practitioners. He observes that 'managers and academics sometimes seem to live in two different worlds, and speak two different languages'. He sees this divide as an 'unfortunate fence . . . which needs to be broken down' (1994, p. 2).

Watson carried out a year-long ethnographic study of the management at a single manufacturing site of a large British telecommunications company, ZTC Ryland. Watson sees managers not just as practitioners but also as theorists. One of his key objectives is to 'bring out the theoretical thinking which lies beneath the surface of the practical activity of managerial work' (1994, p. 2).

ZTC Ryland's managers nominated the ability to be in control and to exercise influence as the things they liked most about being a manager. When these elements were present they described their work using terms like 'I love my job' and 'I absolutely love being here' (1994, pp. 69–70). When asked how free they felt to exercise control in their jobs they responded very positively with comments like 'As free as I want to be', 'So far, very free', 'Totally', '99 per cent' (1994, p. 70).

However, when asked about what they disliked about their jobs it became apparent that they often didn't feel very free at all. Many managers felt great frustration that structural or cultural issues, or the 'bureaucracy', continually got in their way. One manager commented that his greatest struggle was 'the fight to be allowed to manage' (1994, p. 133).

Watson found that a discourse of empowerment, skills and growth coexisted with a rival discourse of control, jobs and costs. While the official culture was informed by the empowerment discourse, 'the unofficial or actual discourse involves an oddly confused mixture' of the two (1994, p. 114).

These following statements demonstrate how these rival discourses resulted in the workplace showing up in an anomalous way for one senior manager:

> I don't shirk at having to make people redundant, I've been doing it for God knows how long. But do we have to just keep doing what someone else decides? I really wonder whether we are valued at all. . . . Do the people running this company realise what we all put into this? What about my empowerment? What about my personal development?
>
> (Watson 1994, p. 119)

Another departmental manager voiced similar sentiments:

> How the hell can you preach this flexibility, this personal and business development at the same time as you are getting rid? As someone said to me yesterday, an operator, 'Why am I in here now doing the best I can getting this product out when tomorrow morning you can give me a brown envelope?' I had no answer . . . This is dangerous – raising expectations and then smashing them . . . Any business has got to keep faith with all of those it deals with if it is going to deserve to survive.
>
> (Watson 1994, pp. 207–08)

Anomaly surfaces from the interplay of the rhetoric and reality that these managers live with. Implicit in the words of both managers is a belief that senior management has broken faith with them and their staff. The 'empowerment, skills and growth' discourse is revealed as another form of control when senior management resumes control of all decision making. At this point, talk of wanting departmental managers to 'manage the business' must appear hollow at best. The second manager's response to his employee's question about the brown envelope reveals his inability to make sense of the anomaly borne from the interplay of these competing discourses, either for himself, or for the worker.

Watson's account captures beautifully the angst and frustration of Ryland's managers as they encounter anomaly, but Watson does not himself notice this as anomaly. He records the following outburst from one such manager:

> I bet you've never seen anything like this outfit. There's so much potential here. But we have this knack of throwing it all away. Every time we decide to go for something we get ourselves all psyched up. We take aim. And then we shoot ourselves in the foot. Why? Tell me why?
>
> (Watson 1994, p. 134)

Watson does not reveal what he said in response but writes, 'This was not an easy question to answer' before going on to suggest:

> The events and the problems in ZTC Ryland present a powerful illustration of the tendency by which the means chosen by the managers of all organisations to achieve certain ends can come to subvert them, rather than serve them.
>
> (Watson 1994, p. 134)

Watson stands with managers as they struggle to make sense of rival discourses of empowerment and control. He hears them as they 'really wonder whether we are valued at all'. But while his critical ethnographic approach leads him to describe what it is like for the managers to practice in the midst of anomaly, it doesn't allow him to see or deal with the anomaly. He sees the complexities and frustrations experienced by these managers not as anomaly, but simply as evidence of his claim that 'management is at the same time both simple in principle and difficult in practice' (1994, p. 10).

At the beginning of this chapter I said that humans like to make sense of things. Gadamer's hermeneutics suggests that coming to an understanding requires one to dwell in the space between the familiar and the strange. I have attempted to describe, both from my own experiences and using Watson's account of management at ZTC Ryland, what it might be like to practise management in a workplace that is simultaneously familiar and strange.

The experience of anomaly is central to this description. However the concept of anomaly or strangeness is absent from Watson's understanding of management practice. Even though Watson is 'embedded' with his manager subjects, his methodology places him outside their experience. Watson concludes by defining management as 'a rather basic human social process' and 'a very practical, down to earth activity . . . (which) seems complex because it involves people' (1994, p. 215). Watson's theory of what it means to be a manager has survived intact. Watson does not experience anomaly as he watches his subjects struggle. He does not see this as an opportunity to reflect on his own practice.

Karl Weick: The Role of Interruption in the Development of Better Theories of Management

The work of Karl Weick (2003) is an example of an academic approach to management practice that acknowledges the valuable insights afforded by experiences of anomaly and how these insights might be used to improve theories about management.

Weick examines the tension between theory and practice and between theorists and practitioners. In discussing the nature of practice and its relationship to theory, Weick draws on Kierkegaard's criticism of philosophers:

> It is perfectly true, as philosophers say, that life must be understood backwards. But they forget the other proposition, that it must be lived forwards.
>
> (Weick 2003, p. 454)

'Living forwards' is a fundamentally different activity to 'understanding backwards'. When human beings are 'living forwards' they are engrossed in their world, absorbed in practical activity. They are not detached and objective. Weick likens 'living forwards' to the Heideggerian concept of thrownness. Winograd and Flores (1986) explain thrownness as being thrown onto one's instincts, forced to act without the benefit of a stable representation of the situation into which one is thrown. One does not have the opportunity to reflect before acting and can't know what the consequences of one's actions might be. One is flying blind but must fly on regardless.

When 'living forwards' is analysed and processed into theory much of this complexity is lost. The end result of this 'understanding backwards' notion is a theory that presents a significantly more orderly representation of practice than the person involved in 'living forwards' experienced. Weick notes that the practitioner's response is to 'complain that no-one is addressing the real world' (2003, p. 453).

The starting point for understanding this gap between 'living forwards' and 'understanding backwards' 'should not be the assumption that people are detached, contemplative, and theoretical, but rather that they are involved, concerned and practical' (Weick 2003, p. 467).

Weick breaks 'living forwards' down into two Heideggerian concepts: 'ready-to-hand' and 'unready-to-hand' (2003, pp. 467–468). When practitioners are engaged in 'ready-to-hand' activity they are in a mode of absorbed coping. They do not grasp their practice theoretically, nor do they see the equipment they use apart from its usefulness in the context within which they are situated.

Practitioners experience an 'unready-to-hand' moment when their absorbed, practical activity is interrupted and their way of 'living forwards' appears to stop working. In these moments of interruption, the practitioner gains a wider perspective on their way of working. Aspects of their situated activity that were previously in the background now show up as issues for the practitioner to think about and resolve in the context of their current ongoing project. The practitioner tends to address these issues as objects to be thought about free of context when they step back from their absorbed practical activity. Heidegger calls this way of being, 'present-at-hand', and it is in this mode, Weick says, that theorising occurs. He restates Kierkegaard using Heidegger's terms:

> Philosophers may be right that life is explained using present-at-hand images, but what they forget is that these images simplify the prior understandings embedded in ready-to-hand living.
>
> (Weick 2003, p. 468)

Weick argues that 'unready-to-hand' moments provide the opportunities for both practitioners and theorists. In these moments practitioners see elements of their practice and context that were previously hidden from view, enabling them to develop a more detailed picture of their way of being in 'ready-to-hand' mode. Weick argues that if theorists can tap into the insights practitioners gain in these 'unready-to-hand' moments, they can use them to develop better theories (2003, p. 469).

Weick's ambition can be understood in terms of Gadamer's hermeneutics. For Gadamer a basic hermeneutic principal is that 'we must understand the whole in terms of the detail and the detail in terms of the whole' (2013, p. 302). If we view those developing management theory as concerned with the whole, and management practitioners as absorbed in the detail, we can see how the establishment of a dialogue between these parties is not only helpful, but essential to the development of a correct understanding of what management is.

Unfortunately the realisation of Weick's ambition is hindered by our current practices for the development of theoretical knowledge. The theorist is not the one experiencing the 'unready-to-hand' moment. This opportunity is afforded to the practitioner. An academic who wants to conduct research into a particular 'unready-to-hand' moment in an organisation needs to find funding, gain permission from the organisation's bureaucracy and obtain ethics clearance. In the meantime, the practitioners are continuing with their living forwards. They are experiencing 'unready-to-hand' moments, reflecting on their practice in 'present-at-hand' mode and resuming their projects. In short, they are doing their own theorising in real time.

The primary concern for both Weick and Watson is with management theory. Watson wants to explain in theoretical terms what it is that managers are doing when they are engaged in the practical activity of management. He is specifically concerned to explain this using language that managers can understand. Weick wants to use experiences of anomaly to improve management theory. This is his response to the criticism from management practitioners that academics are not addressing the real world.

Weick's ambition is admirable and necessary, as is Watson's desire to break down the barriers between management academics and practitioners. It is essential that managers get all of the support possible to equip them for the difficult task of competently managing their organisations. Better management theory is an important part of this. However it is important to understand that the new and improved theory is a long time in development and arrives too late to help the manager struggling to come to terms with his or her way of managing in the midst of an experience of anomaly. Managers need something else besides better theories. They need practical skills that will enable them to make sense of their practice while 'living forwards', especially during times when they experience 'unready-to-hand' moments.

The following section introduces the work of Fernando Flores, Charles Spinosa and Hubert Dreyfus. This work makes an important contribution to the development of practical skills for coping with the experience of anomaly in the workplace.

Fernando Flores: A Manager's Response to Anomaly in the Workplace

Like Kuhn, Fernando Flores (2000) talks of anomaly showing up for the individual against a background of expectation. He uses his own experience as a manager as an exemplar for how anomaly can be used to transform business practices.[1]

While Flores was working as a manager he found that he spent his time working at tasks that did not resemble the tasks he thought he should be performing. Furthermore, these tasks did not seem to add up to anything substantial. He calls these tasks 'disharmonious practices' and these types of anomalies he calls 'disharmonies'. His response to the anomaly was to actively keep doing his task while keeping an eye out for the anomaly.

---

1 This is a reading that emerges out of the work of Spinosa et al. 1997.

Then, when the anomaly arose, he would 'hold onto it' as an anomaly. As a result of this activity, he eventually realised that his anomaly was actually the central feature of his work.

Viewing work as primarily about production or craftsmanship no longer made sense to Flores. Rather, the central feature of work was becoming the coordination of human activity. This was not command and control by another name. Flores realised that work is based on enabling conversations to occur where relationships are established and promises to complete a task are made. For Flores, work is about making and keeping commitments in the context of relationships.

This is an important revelation in the context of our attempts to come to a better understanding of what management is. If work is fundamentally about relationships and promise keeping then perhaps managing work has something to do with managing relationships and building trust between people in organisations. A lack of trust and the breakdown of relationships between middle and senior management was certainly an important factor the tensions at ZTC Ryland.

Using the Experience of Anomaly to Reconfigure our Practices

Flores' approach to dealing with disharmonies is detailed by Spinosa et al. (1997). They base their concept of disharmony on Kuhn's anomaly. Dealing with disharmony requires that one sense and to then hold onto an anomaly, or disharmony, in our practice. This is not a reflective, intellectual activity. Instead of stepping back to analyse the situation, it demands intense practical engagement. 'The best way to explore disharmonies, in other words, is not by detached deliberation but by involved experimentation' (Spinosa et al. 1997, p. 24).

The point of this is to enable the person to use their disharmony to reconfigure their practice in such a way that the disharmony no longer shows up, but rather forms the central feature of the new way of practising. Spinosa et al. are not trying to set out a new theory or produce knowledge. They are attempting to develop sensitivities.

> Once one has a sensitivity to something . . . one is already on the path of refining and developing that sensitivity . . . As one is drawn, time and again, one continuously develops one's skills for dealing with what one is sensitive to.
>
> (Spinosa et al. 1997, p. 39)

As Spinosa et al. suggest, dealing with anomalies is not about looking for a theory that we can use to solve a problem. It calls for developing a way of being and working that will enable us to cope with the thing to which we are sensitive.

Flores took his new conception of work and made it the basis of an enterprise by forming it into a marketable product. This product was a computer software program that helped people coordinate their activities. In this way Flores sought to reconfigure shared practices in the businesses to which he consulted. He didn't use the anomaly to reconfigure the practices of the organisation within which he was a manager. Instead he ceased to be a manager and became an entrepreneur. The enterprise he established to market this new product was based on this new conception of work.

The business strategy Flores' enterprise was based on Spinosa et al.'s approach for dealing with disharmonies. He helped his clients develop their sensitivity to what was disharmonious in their work practices. Then, using his software program as a supporting tool, he enabled the client to reconfigure the shared practices people used for working together collaboratively in their organisation.

It is important to note Flores' ultimate response to his anomaly, while a perfectly valid one for an entrepreneur, is not overly helpful to management practitioners. Flores himself identifies the making and keeping of commitments in the context of relationships as a fundamental aspect of work in organisations. As we have seen from Kuhn's work the presence of an anomaly can lead to the disruption of 'normal' practice. Weick also makes this point when discussing 'unready-to-hand' moments. In these moments it becomes difficult to make sense of things and people's ways of working together can begin to break down. The manager who is sensitive to the anomaly is in a precarious situation. As Kuhn points out, a scientist who pursues an anomaly and brings it out into the open risks his relationship with, and membership of, the community of scientists which have, up until this point, made his or her scientific practice possible. Similarly, managers who draw attention to disharmonies or anomalies in workplace practices put their relationships within that workplace at risk.

One of the challenges of being a manager is trying to deal with the pressures of coordinating groups of people to meet their commitments to each other and to their customers while their ways of working together are breaking down. In my own experience detailed earlier, this was a challenge that ultimately proved too difficult for me. This is a description of 'living forwards'. This is what it means to be 'thrown on your instincts'. Spinosa et al. suggest that the way to deal with these uncomfortable situations is to remain engaged. What follows is a description of how managers might be able to do that.

A Methodology for Practising Management in the Midst of Anomaly

How are we to deal with our 'unready-to-hand' moments at work when we can't call in a consultant or an academic? Even if we could, would it be any help? In the case of the managers at ZTC Ryland, having the academic to talk to simply made the managers conscious of their inability to reconfigure their anomalous practices. That these managers displayed an openness to working with anomaly is evident in comments such as:

> I just don't think we are getting it together. But why aren't we? We do all the right things . . . We should be one of these so-called 'excellent' companies. But I don't think we are.
>
> (Watson 1994, p. 9)

> How the hell can you preach this flexibility, this personal and business development at the same time as you are getting rid?
>
> (Watson 1994, p. 207)

> Every time we decide to go for something we get ourselves all psyched up. We take aim. And then we shoot ourselves in the foot. Why? Tell me why?
>
> (Watson 1994, p. 134)

Watson's approach does not provide the managers with a way of holding on to and working with the anomalies evident in these accounts of their experience. Many of these managers left the company in frustration. What is required is a way for the managers and workers engaged in the work of the organisation to 'hold onto anomalies' (Spinosa et al. 1997, p. 22) as they emerge and to engage in 'involved experimentation' (Spinosa et al. 1997, p. 24).

What follows is an example of involved experimentation in the face of anomaly in the workplace. Once again it is drawn from my own experience.

An Example of Working with Anomaly to Open Up New Ways of Seeing and Being in the World

At the same time I returned to study for a Master of Management degree, I was asked by my old manager to return on a three-month contract to look at the Operations division's on-time performance reporting. He was under pressure from the Sales division to explain a rising number of complaints from customers. These complaints were at odds with the division's reporting which had on-time delivery performance of around 90 per cent every week. He had committed to carrying out a thorough review by an independent analyst from outside his division. I agreed to do it.

As mentioned earlier I had been responsible for the completion of this type of audit in my previous management role. This time around I did the work myself, completing four separate audits over a 12-week period. Like previous audits I was checking that any delivery date changes were done in accordance with approved guidelines. I also looked at the effectiveness of using on-time delivery measures as a performance indicator.

The findings of the audit into date changes were much the same as the results of the audits I presented when I had worked for the company previously, but the analysis into the effectiveness of the on-time performance measure started a chain of events that led to the abolition of date changes and a total restructure of the Operations division.

In shifting the focus away from process compliance I was able to engage people in a broader discussion about their work practices as they related to the things the division and the company said were important. High on the list were customer satisfaction and company profitability.

Operations' contribution to profitability came from the number of services they delivered in a set period of time using a given amount of resources. The 12-week audit found that Operations were delivering only 58 per cent of orders due each week. The remaining 42 per cent of orders were being rescheduled for delivery at a later date. This was causing two problems in relation to profitability. A significant amount of potential revenue was sacrificed. On the day a service is delivered to a customer, it begins to earn revenue for the company. This revenue stream continues until the customer cancels the service. Every day the delivery of the service is delayed represents a day's lost revenue. The second problem was that the total number of orders in the system grew, which had the effect of increasing Operations' administration costs.

I prepared analysis showing that Operations' delivery times were almost double what was promised. I linked this finding to the company's customer satisfaction survey results that rated the company very poorly for meeting service delivery commitments. In terms of profitability, the company was missing out of 17 days' worth of revenue for every service delivered.

In preparing this analysis I worked closely with the division's reporting department. The reporting staff had not been asked to perform this type of analysis before but they were not surprised at the results. In contrast, when I shared the data with the general manager in charge of this department his first reaction was 'this is a load of bullshit'. He asked the reporting staff recheck the data. On learning that the results were genuine his response was 'this report will never see the light of day'.

I also shared the findings with the general manager responsible for the delivery of services to the bulk of the company's business customers. He was highly sceptical of the difference between promised and actual delivery lead-times. He said, 'Sales are obviously promising unrealistic delivery dates so the customers sign up. Then we end up looking bad when we can't deliver.' I explained that this was not that case. Operations' staff were entering orders with a standard delivery lead-time and informing Sales of the delivery date which they then passed on to the customer. The general manager was sceptical and asked the Reporting department to check this.

Once again the analysis was confirmed as correct. The response from the general manager was, 'Shit!'

I also spoke with this manager about the issue of late orders. I gave him a scenario to consider:

> 'You have two orders in front of you that are ready for completion but you only have enough time left today to complete one of them. The first order is due today. The second order is one week overdue. Which order do you tell your people to do?'
>
> He answers immediately, 'Both.'
>
> 'No, seriously,' I say, 'which one do you do?'
>
> 'Seriously,' he says, 'both.'

At this point I had so many things I wanted to say. How can this be? How can this senior manager offer such a useless piece of direction? Operations' *raison d'etre* is the delivery of services to customers. How can it be that in this important matter of prioritising which orders get delivered first, he would offer an impossible solution? What sort of leadership was this? It was at this point that I became aware that my concern was not with the performance measure. I couldn't understand what the purpose of management was in this context.

I didn't share any of these thoughts with the general manager. Instead I went down the line and posed the same scenario to team leaders and front-line staff. They all said the same thing. They would do the order due today ahead of the one due last week. Most, but not all, said they felt this was not fair on the customer whose order was late, but that their priority according to senior management was to look after performance. These individuals often said they would try to get to the late order the next day but that in their experience they would probably end up in the same situation again.

It was during these conversations that another disturbing practice came to light. Some of the teams I spoke with said that their priorities were to do orders due today first and then, if they had any time left over, to start work on orders due tomorrow. Only once these were done would they start on the late orders. In some teams the practice was to 'try to get a couple of days ahead'.

I had begun this process questioning whether or not staff were 'cooking the books' to make their performance look better than it really was. However, at this stage of the process I was concerned with the effectiveness of the measure to manage performance at all. But primarily I was now concerned with management behaviour in guiding the performance of the Operations division.

All of these issues came closest to the surface when discussing the issue of prioritising between due and late orders. It seems such an obvious thing that the customer who has been waiting the longest should get served first. When the choice was put to people in this way they always landed on the side of delivering the due order first. Some managed it without concern, while others were obviously quite uncomfortable about it. When the general manager in charge of all of these people chose not to deal with this complexity, he effectively left it up to his staff to sort it out themselves. In doing so he gave up control of the operation. His staff chose to look after the on-time performance. As a result the average delivery times for customer services increased, a significant amount of potential revenue was lost each week and the number of past due orders increased by the week.

My specific brief at the commencement of this contract was to review the behaviour of Operations' staff in relation to delivery date changes, and whether or not the excellent on-time performance figures were accurate. My approach to this task can be understood in terms of Spinosa et al.'s 'involved experimentation'. I had returned to my old workplace and been asked to deal with the very issue which had caused me, more than any other, to question my ability to be a manager. This issue was, in Kuhnian terms, the source of my anomaly. My way of dealing with the anomaly this time around was to open up a discussion around it. I did this by asking questions. In my questioning I was going about the work I had been contracted to do while remaining sensitive to the anomaly. I was acting as Flores did in his account of his workplace experience of anomaly. I was on the lookout for situations where the anomaly appeared. When the anomaly appeared, I held on to it and questioned further.

I engaged senior management in a discussion about how long it took us to deliver a service to a customer. I gave them the numbers that showed we were taking, on average, twice as long as promised to deliver. I gave them the information from the customer satisfaction survey that showed how dissatisfied our customers were with the length of time we took to deliver services. In light of this information it no longer made sense to talk about delivery date changes and on-time performance. This information evoked strong responses from senior management. It was calling Operations' management practices into question. How could they be reporting delivering 95 per cent of services on-time every week, while at the same time taking twice as long as promised to deliver those services? This information became a source of anomaly for Operations' senior management.

The second example of 'involved experimentation' in the face of anomaly involved the prioritising of orders due today over late orders. In my initial question to the general manager I was attempting to understand how this problem was managed day to day. This manager's unwillingness to choose threw more questions up for me. This led me to involve his staff in the discussion of this issue, from middle managers to front-line managers and staff. All these people were able to choose, but most said they were uncomfortable with their choice. This line of questioning brought their practices into the foreground where they could see them as inconsistent with their values of fairness and providing good customer service.

My final written report included a detailed discussion of these two issues. By questioning what I saw as Operations' anomalous practices around the delivery of customer services, more people had been drawn into a discussion about the sensibleness of their 'commonsense' practices. At this point my contract ended and I left the company.

Three months later I was asked back to help with a restructure of the Operations division. I understood this as the beginnings of Operations' will-ingness to work with anomaly. To use Flores' term, I was being asked by the Operations division to 'hold on to the anomaly' for them. In time this led to Operations developing their own sensitivity to the anomaly and their own way of working with it. An account of this is beyond the scope of this chapter.

Questioning, Sensitivity and Involved Experimentation

At the beginning of this chapter I described the process through which my understanding of what management is was called into question. Gadamer explains that an orientation of openness is essential to answering these types of questions:

> For we have seen that to question means to lay open, to place in the open. As against the fixity of opinions, questioning makes the object and all its possibilities fluid.
>
> (Gadamer 2013, pp. 375–76)

This type of questioning invites answers. It represents 'a breach in the smooth front of popular opinion' (Gadamer 2013, p. 374). The account of my experience during the three-month contract shows how questioning in the presence of anomaly can cause this kind of breach, and how the resulting conversations can bring anomaly to the foreground of an increasing number workplace participants. The questions asked of the Operations division and their performance measures led to a dialogue about the division's way of managing. This dialogue enabled Operations to reconfigure their practices.

I suggest that anomalies are occurring in the workplace on a regular basis. Management academics are working on better theoretical approaches to help practitioners deal with the experience of anomaly. However, in the meantime management practitioners are 'living forwards' and experiencing 'unready-to-hand' moments, or anomalies. Staying in and working with anomaly can be a powerful tool for disclosing a new way of working together, and for creating a better set of shared practices. Central to this approach is the rec-ommendation of Spinosa et al. that we develop a sensitivity to anomaly in our practice.

There are practical steps that practitioners can take to develop these skills. The most obvious is practice. Practitioners need to do what Flores did when he encountered anomaly. They need to get into the habit of dwelling in that uncomfortable territory of not knowing what the solution is. They must resist the urge to find and fix the problem. Instead they must endeavour to *see* the problem. If they seek out and facilitate dialogue among the people in the organisation who are living with the problem on a daily basis they will create opportunities for dialogue and for the development of a shared understanding of the anomaly.

This approach to dealing with the experience of anomaly in the workplace is not about theory or process. In keeping with Flores' revelation about the fundamental nature of work, this approach is relational. I opened this chapter with the statement that humans like to make sense of the world and that they like to do it together. Effective management in the midst of the experience of an anomaly involves the creation of an environment where managers, team leaders and team members can dwell in the midst of the confusion and experiment with ways of making sense of it together.

Finally I come to the problem of Tony Watson's 'unfortunate fence'. I have sought to bring out and hold in tension the uneasy relationship between management academics and management practitioners, between the thinkers and the doers. I have focused on identifying the practical skills managers can develop and use in their 'living forwards' at work. As for the 'understanding backwards' or the theory development part, I think that postgraduate management education represents an opportunity for management academics and practitioners to engage together in 'involved experimentation' to develop a better understanding of management practice.

More work needs to be done here. I have attempted to demonstrate how Gadamer's approach to asking questions in the space between familiarity and strangeness could provide the basis of a methodology for practitioners and academics trying to deal with the strange and anomalous aspects of their practice.

References

Flores, F, 2000, 'Heideggerian Thinking and the Transformation of Business Practice' in Wrathall MA and Malpas, J (eds), *Heidegger, Coping and Cognitive Science: Essays in Honor of Hubert Dreyfus, Volume 2*. Cambridge, MIT Press.

Gadamer, HG, 2013, *Truth and Method*. London, Bloomsbury Academic.

Kuhn, T, 1996, *The Structure of Scientific Revolutions*, 3rd edn. Chicago, University of Chicago Press.

Segal, S, 1999, 'The Existential Conditions of Explicitness: An Heideggerian perspective' in *Studies in Continuing Education*, Vol. 21, No. 1., pp. 73–89.

Spinosa, C, Flores, F and Dreyfus, HL, 1997, *Disclosing New Worlds: Entrepreneurship, Democratic Action, and the Cultivation of Solidarity*. Cambridge, MIT Press.

Watson, TJ, 1994, *In Search of Management: Culture, Chaos and Control in Managerial Work*. London, Routledge.

Weick, KE, 2003, 'Theory and Practice in the Real World' in Tsoukas H and Knudsen T (eds), *The Oxford Handbook of Organisational Theory*. New York, Oxford University Press, pp. 453–75.

Winograd, T and Flores, F, 1986, *Understanding Computers and Cognition*. Norwood, Ablex.

Wrathall, MA and Malpas, J (eds), *Heidegger, Coping and Cognitive Science: Essays in Honor of Hubert Dreyfus, Volume 2*. Cambridge, MIT Press, pp. 271–89.

Chapter 3

Moments of Resolve

Existential Challenges of Everyday Working Life

Amanda Mead and Steven Segal

This chapter highlights the importance of the everyday lived experience of managing on the being and becoming of a manager. To look at management through the existential phenomenological prism of lived experience is to contrast it with a scientific view of management that tends to be stuck in ontology of objects, thereby assuming that everything, including management, must have the status of an object. Focusing on management means focusing on the way of being of a manager, the way of developing habits of practice and the way of be-coming a manager. This focus on managing as a lived experience allows inquiry into the felt sense of managing, the relational aspects of managing and how the ways of being of a manager emerge.

Management like most practices, is a difficult phenomenon to grasp in the abstract. Theorizing about management cannot give one the felt sense for managing. This chapter demonstrates that becoming a manager consists not in the grasp of abstract concepts such as planning, controlling and ordering but in the way in which people who are thrown, leap or thrust into the day to day surprises and tensions of managing respond to the hardly perceptible, hardly significant everyday challenges of managing. Because managing (and *not managing*) emerge as ways of responding to situations, and are mutually constitutive, to understand the process of becoming a manager is to understand the ways in which managers respond to the situations and relations into which they are thrown.

This chapter uses the language and perspective of existential philosophers to identify the inescapable transitional and qualitative abyss or chasm that managers, like any other professionals, must cross to become managers or to inhabit managerial ways of being. As discussed by existential philosophers, this is a frightening and testing space. For one does not know how to go forward, yet in order to develop a sense of self-competence, even mastery as a manager, one needs to go forward in relation with others – yet the unfamiliar and unknown are also there to hold one back.

The chapter is divided into five sections. In the first section we will describe some of the existential dimensions of lived experience. In the second section we will focus on a specific kind of lived experience: what Martin Buber calls an 'existential test'. In the third section we will focus on existential tests in the workplace. In the fourth section we will exemplify an existential test through focusing on one of the author's (Amanda) experience as a young manager. While we have no basis for generalizing beyond her example at this stage, our aim is to use her experience of an existential test and the notion of an existential test in general to begin a conversation regarding the significance of understanding management in terms of lived experience. We conclude by calling for further research to be done from the perspective of the lived experience of managing.

Existential Dimensions of Lived Experience

Linda Hill (2003) writes about managers who in the process of becoming a manager have no familiar beacons or conventions of management to rely on. Yet, they need to act and make decisions without knowing what to do. Hill gives the following example: 'They (managers in her study) were responsible for the lives of others, yet they had to make decisions and act before they understood what they were supposed to do' (Hill, 2003 p. 67). They developed a felt sense for managing in the act of managing and their narrative about self develops through these processes.

The act of managing is inherently a relational one, where self is constantly in interaction with others (Gergen, 2009). Goffman's (2005), view that interaction is about 'Not then, men and their moments. Rather, moments and their men' (p. 3) takes into account the importance of the choices that we make and the actions that we take in interaction as integral to self. Sartre (1973) noted 'of all the actions a man may take in order to create himself as he wills to be, there is not one which is not creative, at the same time, of an image of man such as he believes he ought to be' (p. 29). The idea that we believe we should be a certain way in the world is related to our values and the interactions and social experiences we have relating to those. Many scholars have discussed these aspects of becoming and felt sense of identity including Goffman (1974) who described felt identity or sense of self as a 'subjective sense of his own situation and as the sense of existential continuity coming from social experiences' (p. 105); and Hitlin (2003) who described the 'core of personal identity as being composed of particular value structures' (p. 132).

This chapter is concerned with the process of becoming a manager. Linda Hill (2003) compares the lived experience of becoming a manager to becoming a parent: no matter how much one has read in advance, when the child is upset, crying on your lap, you do not as a new parent have the felt sense how to respond. You feel thrown! However, as you respond, you begin to inhabit the way of being of a parent. Your identity as mother, father or caretaker develops as you respond to the upset baby on your lap. Similarly with management: As the challenges are thrust into your lap, your way of responding, as a manager, begin to emerge.

The words, thrown, thrust and leap should, for those who are familiar, serve as clues to the philosophical framework that will define the focus of this chapter. Existential philosophers like Heidegger write of the notion of being 'thrown' or finding oneself in a situation not of one's own choosing but to which one needs to respond. Buber writes of the psychological and moral responsibility to respond to situations in which one has been thrown. And Kierkegaard (1980) writes of the 'leap' that is required in responding to a situation in which one is thrown. Although Kierkegaard's notion of leaping is often identified as a leap into faith, this is a fallacy. It is arguable that Kierkegaard did not ever speak of a leap into faith. He did speak about leaping – particularly in the context of qualitative transitions in life styles where one cannot rely on logic or any objective reality as a guide. Furthermore, rather than writing of leaps into faith, it was much more the faith of leaping that he was concerned with. The faith of leaping occurs in all those kinds of situations where one has neither experiential nor habitual knowledge of what do not next; yet one is challenged to leap into the abyss, to act.

In this sense becoming a manager involves a series of what Martin Buber calls 'existential tests' (see Hodes, 1998), those tests which cannot be anticipated in advance, cannot be calculated or deliberated upon in abstraction, require responding before thought even intervenes, in which one's identity is being formed and which is the basis of self-worth or lack thereof – depending on how one responds.

This point is central to all existential philosophers. Paraphrasing Sartre, for example, it can be said that only as a manager acts, do they become a manager. There is no way of being called a manager before the acts of managing. It is the acts of managing that establish the embodied practice of managing. Paraphrasing him one step further, no one is born a manager but becomes so through the acts performed.

Similarly, paraphrasing Heidegger, it can be said that the essence of managing lies in its existence. This latter phrase means that it is only through struggling through the lived experiences of managing that managing occurs. Or as Aristotle said, over 2,000 years ago a practice is established through a leap into its performance. It is a process of leaping because the rules are only established as a consequence of and not in advance of the process of leaping. There are no rules guiding this leap. The rules or the habits of practice emerge only through the leap.

However, managing does not follow automatically from lived experience. It could be that the potential manager responds to the uncertainty of lived experience by recoiling or refusing to act or make a decision. This is called 'bad faith' or 'inauthenticity' in existential terms. Bad faith or inauthenticity occur where instead of making a decision in a situation into which a potential manager is thrown, there is an attempt to make as if there are prescribed rules or formulae to follow. And instead of being answerable for decisions being made, one tries to explain them through rules. Instead of owning responsibility for decisions, there is an attempt to rationalize them. It is like the child who constantly comes late for school and blames the timing of the bus.

Sartre's (1973) defence of existentialism argues that every man is 'in possession of himself as he is and places the entire responsibility for his existence squarely upon his own shoulders' (p. 29). However, rather than being a responsibility only to himself, this responsibility is also to and before others. Sartre notes 'in choosing for himself he chooses for all men. For in effect, of all the actions a man may take in order to create himself as he wills to be, there is not one which is not creative, at the same time, of an image of man such as he believes he ought to be' (p. 29). Although Sartre later came to disavow this statement, one of its crucial connotations is that every time we act, we are contributing to setting up a habit of practice through which others travel in establishing their way of being.

Sartre's (1973), notion of 'for all men' means we develop, through our choices, values about how humans 'should' act. We make a statement about how one ought to exist. From a Sartrian perspective, rather than being guided by a prior sense of moral understandings of right and wrong, these moral understandings and principles emerge through choices which in turn influence our sense of self and moral identity. We are formed by the choices that we make. Sartre calls this existential responsibility. These choices and our interpretation of them form our values and become part of our narrative and sense of self. As Oliver Sacks (1998) noted, 'we have, each of us, a life-story, an inner narrative – whose continuity, whose sense, is our lives. It might be said that each of us constructs and lives a "narrative", and that this narrative is us, our identities' (p. 57). This narrative is an inner dialogue that underpins and informs the actions of an individual in all the contexts of their lives.

Responsibility then, from an existential perspective, refers to the way in which a person takes ownership for their way of responding in a situation. Instead of blaming circumstances and thus seeing oneself as a victim of them, responsibility is key to being attuned to and being present in a situation. Rather than sitting back, it allows one to see the possibilities in a situation and thus to be open to unexpected ways of dealing with it. Furthermore, responsibility has an ontological or what we shall call a psychological twist. Our identities are formed through the way we do or do not take responsibility in and for a situation. Responsibility, the choices we own up to making in a situation, transform us. They are the basis of our self-worth or character development – or lack thereof. We become the people that we are through the way in which we take responsibility for our situations. This theme will become clear once the two examples of the chapter are elaborated.

Finally it needs to be said that none of these existential dimensions of becoming a manager are deliberate in a rational and representational sense of the word, that is, we do not first encounter a situation, then stand back from it, think about it from a distance and then implement it. It is a thinking and responding in the context of action, a thinking before any kind of deliberate thought or planning has intervened.

Therefore the existential dimensions of lived experience and the emergent process of becoming involves being thrown into a relational and mutually constitutive situation that is unknown and having to think and respond in the context of action. It also involves taking responsibility (or not) in and for the situation that faces us through the lived experience of the unknown. The authenticity (or lack thereof) of our response will make the action self-affirming or self-negating. But crucial to an existential perspective is that we do not know this narrative in advance of action. For it is only through choosing in action that the narrative of self forms.

Martin Buber's Notion of an Existential Test

Martin Buber's (Hodes, 1998) conceptualization of an existential challenge considers the way in which we make these choices. His view is that self-affirmation and self-negation occur in moments of spontaneous response to an unexpected and anxiety filled situation. We have no time to reflect and no prior knowledge of the consequence of our response, we simply respond, completely as ourselves. It is only in the aftermath that we can reflect on the moment of our true response to the existential challenge. Buber argues that our moral self, our sense of self and philosophy of leading and life develops in these processes.

Buber's (Hodes, 1998, p. 16) example of an existential challenge describes a moment where not only was the person's sense of self at stake, but their very existence was at stake. He discussed the experience of a young medic treating an elderly civilian beside his ambulance in the context of a war. Two heavily armed soldiers 'demanded that the medic release the old man to them' (Segal, 2014 p. 5). The medic was terrified of the soldiers but surprised himself and the soldiers by refusing, telling them, 'This is a first-aid station. . . . I am in charge here. Please go away' (Hodes, 1998, p. 18). The medic would not compromise his protection of the elderly man, even after being threatened with a court martial and then his own life being threatened (Segal, 2014). He stood his ground and eventually the soldiers left. The medic made a choice-in-action, saying, 'If I failed him I would have failed myself' (Hodes, 1998, p. 20).

These choices-in-action are ones in which we have no advanced time to think, no objective rationality to guide us but need to choose without certainty as to the outcome or to how we will be affected by the choice. They are moments in which we let go of the need for security and leap into a future that will emerge only through the choice-in-action.

One of the questions this raises is: what was it like for the medic to behave that way, to act as a leader, to create the future by leaping into it (Segal, 2014, p. 6)?

Even without foundation or convention, there are many ways we bring the sum of our knowledge to every challenge and that helps up determine how to act. Gigerenzer (2007) defined a 'gut feeling' as a judgement appearing quickly in consciousness, whose underlying reason we are not fully aware of and which is strong enough to act upon. Indeed the reason only emerges through the action. Polanyi (1958) asserted that 'into every act of knowing there enters a passionate contribution of the person knowing what is known' (p. viii). Dreyfus (2005) in his discussion of Heidegger talks about 'anticipatory resoluteness', a preparedness and a kind of acceptance and trust in an unknown future that allows the sense of self to emerge (Heidegger, 1967, p. 33).

These experiences in an existential challenge become so important to our sense of self, in part because of the intensity of the emotions experienced. Fredrickson's (2000) evaluations of peak end theory show that 'people's global evaluations of past affective episodes can be well predicted by the affect experienced during just two moments: the moment of peak affect intensity and the ending' (p. 577). Fredrickson (2000) argued that the peaks and ends of an experience may 'be salient precisely because they carry a wealth of self-relevant information. As such, these two moments may in effect become "bouillon cubes" of personal meaning' (p. 593). It is valuable as these moments are rich with self-relevant information, and focusing on them illuminates perceptions of emotions and sense of self (p. 577).

Buber's example describes a very serious and extreme moment where the medic's sense of self and his very existence was at stake. The peak moment of choosing to say no to the soldiers and the end of the experience where he was aware that the soldiers had lost, connect to the medic's values around life and have intense emotions associated with them. This moment when he was tested was an important moment that influenced the rest of his life. He had affirmed himself and gained a stronger sense of who he was from this encounter. He had spontaneously and independently chosen to act as a leader. He had made himself heard in such a way that he achieved the outcome he wanted even though he did not know that would happen. His choices emerged from and impacted on his way of being in the world. He was completely present to the situation and as a consequence of this encounter his self-worth increased and his self-identity as a leader was strengthened.

Existential Tests in the Workplace

Buber's example is very revealing about the nature of the medic's emotions, his presence of mind and the way his self-worth and sense of himself as a leader were developed when he was challenged. However, using such an extreme example diminishes the value of the more ordinary kind of existential challenges, the tests of humanity we all face every day in our lives and workplaces. The small moments where our bonds with humanity are tested, and our response diminishes or affirms our sense of self. These moments where the social bonds are damaged or reinforced happen daily, some are more memorable than others but all are relevant and form part of our personal narrative and sense of self. Examples of the more ordinary kind of existential challenges, the tests of humanity we all face every day in our lives and workplaces are not usually highlighted in practice, but are an important part of self-affirmation and self-negation.

Some of these challenges inevitably happen to managers in the workplace. Work has always been a central feature of the human experience and people's lives are organized and shaped by it. Bolman and Deal (2003) noted that working, as an activity, takes up most of the weekdays and often weekends as well, proportionately more time and energy than given to any other single waking human activity. As a result, work is much more existential than just the simple exchange of time and effort for money. Working and self-affirming interactions with situations and others at work are associated with achievement and status and development of a sense of self. Managing and becoming a manager have become a source of self-respect and identity development.

Workplaces are organized into some kind of social structure and can be more related to an open ecology where people have some capacity for choice; rather than a total institution (Goffman, 2007). In times of corporate change, employees experience self-negation and lose their sense self, of who they are and where they stand in the social structure over extended periods of time. However, employees are tied economically, socially, sometimes geographically and through specialization to their workplace. As a result, in challenging times like a corporate takeover, they often choose to stay with their employer even when their own sense of self is in conflict with the new organizational norms.

Workplaces have only been acknowledged as a place where individual's emotions and sense of self and identity are important in the latter half of the twentieth century. Watson (2008) noted that it is now recognized that moral emotions and feelings pervade every aspect of working and organizational lives. Budd's (2011) concept of work as a social relation inevitably involves emotions and sense of self: 'human interaction embedded in social norms, institutions, and power structures' and, related to that, work as an important part of self and identity, which he defined as 'method for understanding who you are and where you stand in the social structure' (p. 14). This acknowledgement of the inherent relational aspects of managing and the emotional context is reflected in the writings of other organizational scholars such as Fineman (1997), who commented that emotional responses can no longer be considered an 'optional extra' but an integral part of management practices.

The relational act of managing in organizations is enacted, in part, through group interaction in meetings. Social situations like meetings are both the medium and outcome of jointly created events. Self-affirmation and self-negation can accompany each other in these social situations as small test occur; as an analysis of a post-merger organizational meeting where managers were under strong pressure, even coercion to vote in a particular way as their employment was at risk. One manager found it impossible to go against his instincts and sense of responsibility and vote the way he was asked to. His vote against the pressure was a scary leap into faith that may have led to unemployment, but was an emergent experiential response in which he understood his responsibilities and the potential consequences and acted anyway. His action was risky, but was eventually viewed as responsible and necessary dissent and was received positively by his employer. He remained employed at the organization. In his later reflection on the incident, he acknowledged this small moment as an important one of self-affirmation, completely authentic and connected to his personal narrative. Another manager at the same meeting voted against his instincts; at the time trying to explain his actions as a choice he was being told to make, not a real a choice as he felt powerless. Shortly after the incident he left the organization. On later reflection, he noted his discomfort that this incident would always be part of his personal narrative and thus acknowledged the self-negating quality of his action in the vote.

A Managerial Experience of an Existential Test

A more in depth example to illustrate a managerial experience of an existential test is taken from Amanda's lived experience as a young and inexperienced manager. Diary notes from a meeting early in her career, and told in the first person, exemplify opportunities for self-affirmation. In this meeting, she was in a situation where she had no experiential or habitual knowledge of what to do or how to act.

All the participants in the meeting described can be characterized as being involuntarily emotionally committed to the organizational change process. For most of the participants, the changes were unwanted, unwelcomed and imposed upon them. For all the participants, these changes created uncertainty and 'existential anxiety . . . where we feel we can no longer rely on our own way of doing things' (Segal, 2014, p. 247) for all.

> I was in a grand meeting room in a country town. The room was large, with windows overlooking a well-kept garden. The table was large, well polished and big enough to seat twenty people. The chairs, heavy and well padded, were lined up around it like old soldiers on parade. This was a grand room, mostly unused, built over fifty years earlier for successful people to watch over their business in.
>
> As I waited for the managers to arrive, I was nervous. I was the youngest and the only female manager in a company of over three thousand

employees. My organization, over ten times the size of theirs, had just 'merged' with their one. I was an outsider, from Head Office, here to tell them how their brand identity will change over to ours, just one of the changes. The branding and marketing changes were part of the economic basis of the merger and they should already know this. But I had spent the morning in the factory with the workforce and, at least there, they all seemed to think that nothing will change.

I watched them walk in, a group of men in their forties and fifties, experienced, capable and confident in their skills in production, with the kind of weathered faces you see in people who spend a lot of their time outside. We introduced ourselves uncomfortably. I felt slightly defensive. After making sure that they all have the paperwork we all took our seats and I started to take them through the presentation, trying to read the audience response and feeling the tension of being the outsider. The presentation had been ready and rehearsed for months. I tried to project my voice to the other end of the table, but it sounded squeaky inside my head, not confident at all. I watched them watching me.

I got to the timetable for the stages of converting the brand over on packaging when the Factory Manager angrily interrupted saying, 'This is bullshit. The locals will never accept it. You people think you can just walk in and change the place, but you don't know anything.' I breathed deeply and explained that the change was part of the basis of the merger. The managers started to shift in their seats and talk angrily about being lied to. They fell onto rational supports for their point, brand loyalty, local meaning, the costs of change of packaging and signage. They shouted and pointed at me as though I was personally to blame for it. I tried to respond calmly and with logic, but it was pointless in the face of this emotion so I stopped. In my inexperience their reactions seemed excessive. I looked to the ex General Manager for support. He was sitting next to me, an older man, close to retirement. He had known these managers all his working life. He just flushed and wouldn't look at me or them. I felt sick, hot and embarrassed.

I realized that for this group of experienced men the world had shifted on its axis. Their extreme distress and anger seemed to be simply because the brand name on the factory and the products was changing. It did not make sense to me, that they were unable to contain their emotions. But this is/was their grand room, their world, their certainty that had gone. These men were angry and they had to play out this scene in their grand meeting room in front of me, an audience that they probably felt diminished them. But somehow they did not leave, held there by invisible threads that I barely understood. They talked powerfully about being betrayed and angry. They were being thrown into emotions they didn't want to feel. They felt hopeless and abandoned and in some way ashamed. I realized that there must be more to it, something symbolic about it that I had not understood and I wondered why it meant so much.

Thrown into unknown territory, I abandoned the presentation and just sat, listened, there with them, trying to be part of them even though I felt alone and lonely; I wanted to help and but felt useless. I felt there was nothing else I could do but be there. The afternoon went by. The voices got quieter. One of them made a joke and some smiled, some laughed in response. They started to include me in the conversation. The ex General Manager was silent. We started working on the implementation plan.

This type of meeting was unfamiliar to the protagonists and did not seem fit the usual metaphors of a workplace meeting. This scene, so shocking then, was echoed a number of times as the organization 'merged' with many other smaller ones and Amanda's reaction that day became the model for her future interactions. The men in the meeting were experiencing a self-negating sense of worthlessness, powerlessness and exposure, a sense of feeling 'fundamentally bad as a person' (Kaufman, 1974, p. 569). They had turned inward, engrossed in their own experience and less able to focus on others. This is in itself an existential state as even though they may have or have not been aware of the way in which their identity was threatened by the merger, it was affecting the way in which they experienced themselves and the way in which the world was disclosed to them. As Andrew Grove (1996) of Intel says: ' So, when your business gets into serious difficulties, in spite of the best attempts of business schools and management training courses to make you a rational analyzer of data, objective analysis will take second seat to personal and emotional reactions almost everytime' (p. 124).

Heidegger's notion of being 'thrown' or finding oneself in a situation, not of one's own choosing but to which one needs to respond completely, describes Amanda's situation. She was thrown into an unknown space with neither objective nor subjective certainty. Going beyond the rational in change, entering the qualitative lived experience of organizational life is entering an existential space; a space between the collapse of the old and the not yet of the new.

Kierkegaard's faith of leaping into the unknown requires responding to a situation in which one is thrown, where one has neither experiential nor habitual knowledge of what do not next; yet one is challenged to act. Amanda did not know that she would get the very hostile response to the presentation as she thought they already knew about it. Her response, the choice she made, 'allowing chaos to reign and then reigning chaos in' (Grove, 1996), to be silent and abandon the presentation was because she instinctively wanted to help these men and felt responsible for their wellbeing. Their sense of anxiety, perhaps a sense of careers being at stake and an existential aloneness, needed acknowledging honestly before they could begin to move through it.

Sartre's view of individual's psychological and moral responsibility to respond to situations in which one has been thrown is also relevant in this example. In accepting the responsibility Amanda had in the situation, she was compelled to accept it's unfolding without trying to control it. Anything she did to control it would have simply made their experience worse than it already was.

Amanda's felt sense of being alone in the room and feeling lonely was instructive and useful. In line with Moustakas' (1981) observation that 'loneliness exists in it's own right as a source of power and creativity, and as a source of insight and direction' (p. 208), she found herself responding to the situation in an entirely unexpected way. The moment of turning away from the presentation and into relationship with these men disrupted the loneliness for both her and for them. She also knew that her own manager would have reacted very differently and become angry with these men. As she represented him, her response was risky but it felt completely authentic to her. Through this process, she learned that these moments of thrown-ness and anger at their situation and movement to hopelessness to acceptance were helping them rebuild their sense of self and central to their self-identity at work.

This existential challenge seems on the surface to be unlike Buber's example. There was no life or death situation, Amanda was not physically threatened, and the choices she made were not obviously self-affirming. However, like Buber's medic, she did not have any concrete reference point, no conventions she could rely upon, no clear subjective sense of her own situation and no time to think. Amanda did have her own particular value structures about how humans 'should' act, and moral understanding of right and wrong, and an understanding that she had choices.

This was a more ordinary kind of existential challenge or test, the kind of moment of choice and resolve we all face every day in our interactions in our lives and workplaces, embedded in our social norms, institutions and power structures. These are moments of resolve or anticipatory resoluteness, where a preparedness and a kind of acceptance and trust in an unknown future allowed her sense of self to emerge. For Amanda did not know in advance how she was going to respond to the situation. She was nervous, experiencing a kind of anticipatory anxiety. The meeting did not start in the manner she expected. She did not behave the way she thought her manager would behave. Rather her attunement came from inside her and expressed her own voice. She surprised herself by not only being able to stay calm in the 'eye of the storm' but to be attuned, empathetic and authentic.

Twenty years later, Amanda is conscious that her actions that day changed the way she understands herself. Through her choices her sense of self and moral identity were affirmed. Through the 'bouillon cubes' of personal meaning that she remembers, she became more certain that she was the person she wanted to be and, in doing so, became more of that person. This moment of existential challenge became a crucible through which her way of being as a manager was forged. Those men also became more aware of her in that light, and the way she was viewed was changed, because she was changed. This became clearer as they accepted and supported Amanda's move up through the organizational hierarchy. As Sartre (1973) noted, 'Man is nothing else but that which he makes of himself' (p. 28). She remains conscious that on that ordinary working day, that moment was authentic and self-affirming.

Placing this in existential terms, Amanda's way of being as a manager emerged out of the way in which she responded to the situation at hand. Her way of being did not come from a pre-thought out plan, from reading text books, from what one ought to do in such situations but as a pre-reflective response to the situation. For she at no stage stood outside of the conversation like a scientist or Platonic philosopher king to view concerns from an abstract distance. Rather she was fully immersed in the lived experience and responded authentically out of the lived experience, and learnt about herself as a manager out of the way she responded.

Research as Lived Experience

The world of management research largely comes from a scientific perspective and is designed to develop objective and subjective certainties in the workplace. This research is clearly valuable but does not tell the whole story as managers are working with ambiguity and different challenges every day. Managing is a continual process of becoming with small and large challenges or tests creating opportunities for self-affirmation and self-negation through each day.

The small but significant day to day lived experience of managers is the basis of the formation of their identities but this has by and large been under theorized. For lived experience is not a category that fits hand in glove with scientific concepts of management which like to begin, as all sciences do, to focus on the objects of experience rather than the lived experience of objects. Yet, if we listen to the voices of management scholars like Henry Mintzberg and Linda Hill, it is with firsthand experience rather than with management as an object of inquiry that we need to begin. If we need to begin with an appreciation of lived experience, then existential philosophy, as has been demonstrated in the course of this chapter, provides us with a language to describe the lived experience of managing and becoming a manager.

Research on management as lived experience using an existential philosophical framework and Buber's conceptualization of an existential challenge offers a focus on ways of being a manager, managing in practice and the moments where our felt sense of managing and philosophy of leading emerges and act as a crucible where our narrative of self forms.

Furthermore existential research is congruent with professional practice research as it provides a framework for research from within rather than from outside of a field of practice. This was demonstrated to be the case in the example used in this chapter to exemplify and bring out some existential dimensions of managing and of how Amanda became a manager through these experiences. This did not mean that she simply looked into herself or her psyche or personality. Rather it was her way of being or practising as a manager that emerged in this existential form of research. While it might not be accessible in terms of objective criteria of truth, there is no doubt that it forms the basis of an invitation to a thoughtful and reflective conversation for managers own lived experience of managing. As Richard Rorty points out, existential research aims for nothing more: it is not about objective truth but insight, seeing differently and opening up new possibilities – all of which are central to the practice of managing.

References

Bolman, L G and Deal, T E, 2003, *Reframing organizations: Artistry, choice, and leadership*, 3rd edn, Jossey-Bass, San Francisco, CA.

Budd, J W, 2011, *The thought of work*, ILR Press, Ithaca, NY.

Dreyfus, H 2005, 'Can there be a better source of meaning than everyday practices? Reinterpreting Division I of Being and Time in the light of Division II' in *Heidegger's being and time: Critical essays*, Rowman & Littlefield Publishers, Inc. Lanham, MD.

Fineman, S, 1997, 'Emotion and Management Learning', *Management Learning, Volume 28, Issue 1*, pp.13–25.

Fredrickson, B L, 2000, 'Extracting meaning from past affective experiences: The importance of peaks, ends, and specific emotions', *Cognition & Emotion, Volume 14, Issue 4*, pp. 577–606.

Gergen, K J, 2009, *Relational being: Beyond self and community*, Oxford University Press, New York.

Gigerenzer, G, 2007, *Gut feelings: The intelligence of the unconscious*, Viking, New York.

Goffman, E, 1974, *Frame analysis*, Harper and Row, New York.

Goffman, E, 2005, *Interaction ritual: Essays in face-to-face behavior*, Aldine Transaction, New Brunswick, NJ.

Goffman, E, 2007, *Asylums: Essays on the social situation of mental patients and other inmates*, Aldine Transaction, New Brunswick, NJ.

Grove, A S, 1996, *Only the paranoid survive: How to exploit the crisis points that challenge every company and career*, 1st edn, Currency Doubleday, New York.

Heidegger, M, 1967, *Being and time*, Blackwell, Oxford.

Hill, L A, 2003, *Becoming a manager: How new managers master the challenges of leadership*, 2nd edn, Harvard Business School Press, Boston, MA.

Hitlin, S, 2003, 'Values as the core of personal identity: Drawing links between two theories of self', *Social Psychology Quarterly, Volume 66, Issue 2*, Special Issue: Social Identity: Sociological and Social Psychological Perspectives, pp. 118–137.

Hodes, A, 1998, *Encounter with Martin Buber*, Penguin Books, Harmondsworth.

Kaufman, G, 1974, 'The meaning of shame: Toward a self-affirming identity', *Journal of Counseling Psychology, Volume 21, Issue 6*, pp. 568–574.

Kierkegaard, S, 1980, *The concept of anxiety*, Princeton University Press, Princeton, NJ.

Moustakas, C, 1981, 'Heuristic research' in *Human inquiry: A sourcebook of new paradigm research*, P. Reason & J. Rowan, J. Wiley, Chichester, UK and New York, pp. xxiv.

Polanyi, M, 1958, *Personal knowledge: Towards a post-critical philosophy*, University of Chicago Press, Chicago.

Rorty, R, 1980, *Philosophy and the mirror of nature*, Basil Blackwell, Oxford.

Sacks, O, 1998, *The man who mistook his wife for a hat: And other clinical tales*, Simon and Schuster, New York.

Sartre, J-P, 1973, *Existentialism and humanism*, Eyre Methuen, London.

Segal, S, 2014, *Business feel: Leading paradigm shifts in organisations*, Palgrave Macmillan, Basingstoke.

Watson, T J, 2008, *Sociology, work and industry*, 5th edn, Routledge, London.

Chapter 4

Escaping the Iron Triangle
Existential Hermeneutics and the Practice of Project Management

Brad Rolfe

Trapped in the Iron Triangle

The idea of an existential hermeneutic approach to project management practice was not something I arrived at easily, or even very early in my career. By the time I became aware of the possibility of using philosophical theories of interpretation to explore organisational narratives, I had been a project management practitioner in the Australian IT industry for nearly 20 years.

I began my career in the early 1990s, first as a software developer and then gravitated quickly towards the organisational aspects of the work. A steady progression through the 'ranks' of project management followed; technical planner, project co-ordinator, implementation manager (all essentially junior project manager roles) and then project manager. Whilst the titles have changed, and the organisations I have worked for have changed, the essential problem has always remained the same: How to give the stakeholders what they want? In the formal discipline of project management those wants are invariably translated into what was famously coined by Martin Barnes in 1972 as the 'iron triangle' of time, cost and performance.[1] Or, in other words, what do you want, when do you want it by, and how much do you want to pay? All of which sounds relatively simple.

In reality, it is far from simple. It is very, very hard to deliver a project of any reasonable size and complexity in any industry in the contemporary corporate environment. The Standish Group CHAOS Report on IT industry projects in 2009 noted that nearly 70 per cent of projects it reviewed were

---

1 The author attended the 26th IPMA World Congress in Crete in 2012 where Dr Martin Barnes (again a keynote speaker) spoke about how he 'conjured up' the iron triangle for the IPMA World Congress keynote address in 1972 in Stockholm. He noted that in his original presentation he used the terms 'time, cost and quality', but later changed it to 'time, cost and performance', as performance was a better component for capturing the desired outcomes of a project. These desired outcomes could often exceed the specifications implied in the term 'quality'.

either late, over budget or cancelled (Group 2009). A joint study by McKinsey and the BT Centre for Major Program Management on IT projects across a wide range of industries found that 50 per cent of projects with a budget of $15M or over ran at least 45 per cent over budget. They were also delivered 7 per cent behind schedule and delivered 56 per cent less functionality than originally specified (Bloch et al. 2012).

Nor is this problem restricted to the IT sector. In research into large construction projects in over 20 nations, Flyvberg (2012) observed, 'nine out of ten projects have cost overruns. Overruns of over 50% are common, whilst overruns of over 100% are not uncommon'. Most significantly, Flyvbjerg noted, 'overruns have been constant for the seventy years for which data are available, indicating that no improvements in estimating and managing costs have been made over time' (2012:12).[2]

At a personal level, after nearly 15 years as a freelance contractor in the IT industry, moving from one project and company to the next, I was growing increasingly disaffected with the practice in which I was engaged. No amount of effort or technical skill appeared to make a difference to the outcome (Rolfe and Segal 2011). No matter the exhaustive number of requirements that my various project teams gathered, the volumes of project 'artefacts' that we produced or the size and complexity of the ever-expanding schedules that we created, few if any projects could be brought in against their original parameters.

This does not mean that all the projects I ran were considered unsuccessful. Despite the overruns, and the additional budget and the reductions in scope, many stakeholders were satisfied with the project as it was delivered. This only served to make it worse. It was as if I was a doctor and, despite losing the patient, the family were relatively happy with my effort! Such was the level of my dissatisfaction that, in 2005 and after a particularly bad experience running a project for a large government department (a project that ended with me retrenching eight of my colleagues in the course of a single day – the single worst day of my working life), I contemplated turning my back on project management.

The philosopher Alasdair Macintyre (1984) noted that, 'the experts claim to status and reward is fatally undermined when we recognise that he possesses no sound stock of law-like generalisations and when we realise how weak the predictive power available to him is' (p.106) The 'law-like generalisations' of the formal project management discipline, which I had studied through project management manuals such as the *Project Management Body*

---

2 Bent Flyvbjerg: currently Professor of Major Programme Management at Oxford University's Said Business School. As Professor of Planning at Aalborg University, Denmark, his investigations into the massive cost overruns incurred by a number of very large public construction projects ultimately led to him being knighted by the King of Denmark.

of Knowledge (PMBoK)[3] and Prince-2,[4] had revealed their weaknesses to me and left me with me no predictive powers to speak of. I was experiencing a profound disruption to my practice as a project manager, one that no amount of formal training or certification appeared able to resolve. How did I escape the 'iron triangle' of the formal project management method and re-establish an authentic relationship to my practice?

Disruption as the Basis of Existential Hermeneutic Research

It was at this relatively low-point in my career that I began my PhD. At first it had been as an escape from what was the increasing frustration of my work as a project manager. I had become interested in continental philosophy in general and existential hermeneutics in particular whilst doing a research thesis for my MBA, and when the opportunity presented itself to continue in this vein with a doctoral thesis I leapt at it. Whilst it was an endlessly fascinating area of inquiry, I did not at first see the opportunity it afforded for insight into my own practice. I felt project management was a far too practical activity to take advantage of what appeared, at first glance at least, to be the deeply theoretical and intensely abstract philosophical school of existential hermeneutics. It was to the credit of my supervisor, Steven, that I was eventually able to see how wrong I was about both project management and existential hermeneutics. Project management as a deeply human activity is imbued with far more meaning than I ever gave it credit for, and it was the situated, contextual and surprisingly practical field of existential hermeneutics that ultimately allowed me to see that.

It was not until well into my first year of part-time study that I began to see the possibilities of informing my practice with research in an existential hermeneutic mode. Where to begin though? Unlike a quantitative study that many of my fellow researchers were engaged in, I did not have a specific question that would provide the focus of my research. For example, a colleague of mine was conducting research into the relationship between the success of a project based on its originally defined parameters of time, cost and specification, and the perceived stakeholder value of the same project. This kind of question allowed for the possibility of measurement, of comparing one set of data with another and generating some specific conclusions.

By contrast, all I appeared to have was a singular and intense dissatisfaction with my practice. There was no specific question that I was asking.

3 *The Guide to the Project Management Body of Knowledge* (PMBoK), is published by the Project Management Institute. It released the 5th Edition of the standard in 2013.
4 Projects in Controlled Environments [Prince-2] is a non-proprietary project management standard developed by the UK Government.

Instead, my entire working life was itself 'in question' as the everyday activities I conducted (and was still conducting whilst I researched my dissertation) no longer carried the meaning they once had. In fact, I had become so deeply suspicious of the tools of my trade that I viewed them as a carpenter might view a saw that he suspects is not cutting straight, or a hammer where the head keeps slipping off. The pivotal moment of my research came with the understanding, gained from the work of Martin Heidegger (1993), that such disruptions to my everyday practice were not an impediment to existential hermeneutic research, but were actually the basis of it.

Heidegger observed that disruption makes everyday activities a theme of explicit concern in their own right: 'when an assignment [activity] has been disturbed – when something is unusable for some purpose – then the assignment becomes explicit' (1996:105). Putting it another way, Hubert Dreyfus noted that, 'normally we do not notice the things that are accessible, we just transparently use them, or notice the difficulty of access to them, but go on anyway. But if there is an obstacle I may have to stop and think about how to reach my goal' (1991:138). My practice as a project manager had been disrupted by my inability to achieve what I considered the goals of the practice. As a result, I had been forced to stop and think about those goals. My practice had, in Heideggerian terms, become explicit for me (Heidegger 1996).

Rather than focus on specific problems *within* the practice, an existential hermeneutic treats the disruption itself as a legitimate area of concern. Disruption implies something other than a simple problem to be resolved. A problem is a piece of wood jamming a door and preventing it from opening. Forcing out the piece of wood or using another door are the possible solutions to this problem. Disruption is not like this. Disruption is when the relationship we have with our everyday activities no longer makes sense. Disruption tests something far more significant than our intellect or our skills, it tests our way of being in the world (Heidegger 1993). This was the manner in which my practice had been disrupted. It was not a problem demanding a solution in the traditional sense, but a problem with my 'way of being' a project manager.

Heidegger (1996) uses the word *Dasein* or 'being there' to describe our way of being in the world. Segal (1999) notes that Heidegger's *Dasein* is not to be confused with our consciousness, or our 'mind'. *Dasein* has no essential structure that precedes our experience of the world, but *is* our experience of the world. Expressed another way, *Dasein* represents a mode of being that is our particular stance towards the world as it appears around us. For the most part, *Dasein* is not explicitly recognised. People are typically so absorbed in day-to-day activities that an awareness of their way of being in the world eludes them. People interact with the world but seldom question the nature of their interaction (Segal 1999). As Heidegger puts it, people normally enjoy a constant state of familiarity with their way of being. It is only when everyday activities are disrupted in some way that this familiarity is challenged

(Heidegger 1996). It is under conditions of disruption that our habitual ways of doing things are rendered explicit and there is an awareness of actually being aware (Segal 1999).

So it was for me. In the early part of my career I was in a state of everyday familiarity with my practice. The projects I was engaged to run by my clients were relatively small and not overly complex. This did not mean they were easy. By and large they were very demanding in the amount of effort required to make them successful. But the path to that success was clear. Early on I completed the necessary certifications offered by the Project Management Institute and found them to relate well to the problems of my practice. I found if you followed their reasonably consistent method and kept everyone else to it as well, the tools did their job and achieved the outcomes that were intended. As a result I had no need to question the practice I was engaged in.

Over time, things began to change. As I became more proficient at my work I was given increasingly more demanding projects to run. This is an entirely normal state of affairs in any practice. What did not occur was a corresponding increase in the level of knowledge that came with that increased responsibility. Beyond the pages of the project management manuals, there seemed little else to guide my activity. As they were laid out, the guides to project management knowledge claimed to 'apply to any project, regardless of size, scope or complexity' (PMI 2013). It was like joining a secret society, only to have every secret revealed on day one, and those secrets were uninspiring at best. Far from gaining mastery of my tools, I found the tools became less and less relevant to the problems with which I was increasingly confronted.

Heidegger remarks that disruption to our everyday activities is frequently revealed as an experience of 'strangeness' (1993:343). In moments of strangeness we become beings who question our particular way of being. Heidegger thinks 'only when the strangeness of what-is forces itself upon us does it awaken and invite our wonder. Only because of wonder . . . does the why [or how come?] spring to our lips. Only because of this "why?" Are we fated to become enquirers' (1993:348). In every questioning it is not just the object or subject matter that is being inquired into but the inquirer themselves. 'Every research question can only be put in such a way that the questioner as such is by his very questioning involved in the question' (1993:325)

The strangeness brought about by disruptions to our everyday routines can challenge more than the way we do things. Arnold and Fischer (1994) point out that sufficient attention to strangeness allows us to 'become aware of new possibilities of what it is to be a human being' (p.56). My experience of strangeness in my practice reflected this observation. It was disruption to my everyday practices and the experience of strangeness it produced that led me to my research. I had no fixed idea of what that research should be or even of what problem I was trying to resolve, but the question of 'why?' had clearly sprung to my lips and was driving my inquiry from within.

Interpreting Experience and 'Breaking in' to the Hermeneutic Circle

Having established disruption and the experience of strangeness as the existential basis of my research, there remained the issue of interpreting the experience to uncover some kind of meaning within it. It was not enough for me to simply acknowledge the disruption and the strangeness. I wanted to explore these experiences and determine if they held the key to a different kind of project management practice.

In Heidegger's perspective, meaning is in no way contained within the objects of our inquiry, but is invested in the relationship we have with them (Heidegger 1996). Accordingly, I could see that the tools of project management held no meaning in and of themselves, but gained their meaning through my relationship to them. Meaning was not an independent entity, capable of being studied from a distance. As the inquirer into my own disruption I was effectively injecting myself into the situation I was attempting to interpret. This is, as Heidegger points out, the only way it can be. We are 'always already' in a situation that we are inescapably a part of (1996:174). As a result, we unavoidably bring our own preconceptions to whatever situation we seek to inquire into. Hermeneutic phenomenology emphasises that our prejudices actually provide the basis for our interpretation rather than constrain it (Arnold and Fischer 1994).

Heidegger claimed that we only have access to the world through an initial understanding of it and our initial understanding is contained in our 'prejudices' or what Heidegger calls a 'pre-thematic' understanding (1996:80). Rather than its typical connotation of a pre-existing negative attitude towards a situation or person, prejudices are what Heidegger refers to as the fore-structure of understanding. A fore-structure of understanding implies that the meaning derived from our understanding is conditioned by the meaning brought to it (Segal 1999). This raises one of the most significant objections to an existential, hermeneutic and phenomenological mode of research: If all understanding is interpretation, and interpretation is framed by an existing pre-understanding contained in our prejudices, how does one ever break out of what is a circular theory of our relationship to the world? (Dreyfus 1991)

I have to admit to being perplexed by this myself. I had been working as a project manager for a very long time and had formed some definite opinions about my practice (not all of them good!). Wouldn't these opinions, coloured as they were by my emotions and my experiences, 'get in the road' of legitimate research? Didn't I first have to set my subjective experiences to one side so I could adequately define the problem? Only then, I thought, would I be in a position to break that problem down, to reduce it to first causes and ultimately solve it.

Heidegger demonstrates the error implicit in this kind of thinking. A reduction to first causes is the aim of the epistemological method of the natural sciences, and it is within the context of the epistemological method that the circularity of cause and effect becomes an issue for us (Heidegger 1993). Hermeneutical phenomenology, Heidegger argues, avoids the so-called 'problem' of the circularity of meaning involved in subjective interpretation, by refusing the necessity to escape from the circle of meaning at all: 'To see a vitiosum [defect] in this circle and to look for ways to avoid it, even to feel that it is an inevitable perfection, is to misunderstand understanding from the ground up' (1966:153) Instead, Segal (1999) proposes that, 'not only does the human being's sense of the world emerge from its activities within the world, but also its sense of self emerges from the ways in which it is involved in the world. It is our involvement in the world that shapes us into the kind of people that we are' (p.80).

The question arising from this for me was: how did I go about breaking into the hermeneutic circle of understanding? At what point in the backwards and forwards between experience–understanding–experience did I begin my research and try to shed light on my practice? If the traditional tools of objective inquiry were inadequate for the kinds of problems that confronted me, what methods were available to me to try and make sense of the disruption I was experiencing?

Focusing and the Felt Sense

Ultimately, the hermeneutic, existential and phenomenological method I settled on for my research was the focusing method outlined by Eugene Gendlin (1981). Explicitly grounded in the philosophy of Martin Heidegger, the method of focusing came about through Gendlin's practice as a psychotherapist and his observation that psychotherapy was effective for some patients and not for others. Gendlin asked himself: what allowed some patients to garner valuable self-insight into their own practices as human beings and make significant improvements to their lives, whilst others languished in endless rounds of therapy and self-doubt? Gendlin's research into this question revealed that those patients who displayed self-insight usually did so within the first two or three sessions. It appeared to make little difference which techniques the therapist applied or what specifically was talked about. What those patients *did inside themselves* made the difference. What those successful patients applied intuitively, Gendlin sought to turn into a skill that could be taught (Gendlin 1996).

The primary aim of the method of focusing is the naming of what Gendlin refers to as the 'felt sense'. The felt sense is a description of the physical sensation of a change or shift in our bodily recognition of our feelings (Gendlin 1981:10). Todres shows how an attention to the 'felt sense' of a problem is an attempt to put to language what the body already knows. 'Credible sense-making involves the emotional relief that happens when words are felt to express the uniqueness of personal experience' (Todres 2007:71) and it is by working through the bodily reactions to our unique personal experiences that words are able to be put to that which had previously escaped description.

Critically, the felt sense is not to be confused with a more general attitude of 'getting in touch with our emotions'. A felt sense is not an emotion. It is a bodily reaction to an experience and is therefore not easily identifiable. Gendlin states 'there are no ready-made words for it in the language so it is hard to describe. Until now very few people understood it [the felt sense]. Society, and thus also language, viewed the only the resulting manifestations – thoughts, emotions, perceptions, – not the felt sense' (Gendlin 1981:7).

The usefulness of the felt sense to both psychotherapy and general research is the complicity of body and language. Focusing on the felt sense recognises that language is an extension of the body and, likewise, the body requires language to become more than itself. Language and the body are not separable or reducible to one another (Todres and Galvin 2008). The complicity between body and language is therefore the foundation of research in the existential hermeneutic phenomenological tradition. 'The lived body, characterised as the messenger of the unsaid, provides possibilities for understanding situations that exceed any precise formulation or patterning of it' (Todres 2007:5).

The focusing technique is invariably (but not always) used in the form of a one-on-one interview. As perhaps the primary tool in qualitative research, the purpose of the interview is to 'understand the experience of other people and the meaning they make of that experience' (Seidman 1991:78). Unlike quantitative information gathering, the interviewer is an adaptable instrument, capable of responding in a multitude of ways to the data that he or she gathers and then re-framing the following questions to suit the direction the research is taking. The process of the interview therefore blurs the distinction between the researcher and the subject of the research. The researcher asks questions of their research subjects and then interprets their responses in light of their own understanding (unavoidably so, Heidegger would argue). This new understanding alters their following questions which in turn elicits a different kind of response and so on. It is a continual interplay as the familiarity of the interviewee is challenged by the questions of the researcher (Todres 2007).

I began my own research journey by exploring the felt sense of my experience of disruption in my practice as a project manager. In this case, my supervisor, Steven, took the role of researcher and interviewed me about my experience of project management. Steven and I worked to articulate the phenomena of disruption using Gendlin's method of focusing.

What became apparent in these interviews was that I had a deep ambivalence towards my practice. I carried the felt sense of this ambivalence in the ambiguity of expressions I used to describe the way I felt about the fragmented and disconnected nature of my work, which involved moving with frequent regularity from one project and organisation to the next. I used both expressions of 'uneasiness', alongside expressions of 'freshness', indicating that whilst I saw this frequent movement as potentially damaging to my sense of professional identity, there was also something exhilarating about it. By 'clearing a space' (Gendlin 1981:52) for my felt sense and not trying to immediately problem solve, this ambivalent attitude towards my work began to emerge. It was as yet unnamed, and therefore evaded the theoretical and conceptual constraints that naming would inevitably bring.

As we progressed, other aspects of my uneasiness became clear. For example, it mattered to me that I struggled to describe my function in an organisation. Once the title of project manager was stripped away, what remained for me were the physical activities performed, and on that count I was no different from a line manager, an accountant or a financier. Indeed, there was little to distinguish me from most other individuals in a corporate setting. There was nothing that appeared to make my role worthy of its own description. The fact remained that I was doing *something* though I couldn't say what that something was. I alluded to the careers of my parents, both recently retired. My father had been an army officer for nearly 30 years and then a senior public servant. My mother had been a primary school teacher for the same period of time. I could not help but compare my working life to theirs, and in doing so found my own career wanting, but for reasons that were still not clear.

In acquiring a handle to the problem, the problem itself may begin to change as different kinds of words come into play and serve to alter perspectives on the felt sense. An example might be an office worker discussing their experience of work. They may use many words to try and capture the 'felt sense' of their experience but occasionally a single word, such as 'drowning' will just feel right and this will be experienced as a bodily 'shift' (Gendlin 1981:56). In a similar way, words such as 'languages', 'game playing' and 'mask' begin to resonate with me. Steven and I toss them back and forth, playing with the words we have uncovered, seeing if any of them are a better fit to the felt sense of my unease. Eventually, I make the observation that:

> I'm sort of a . . . well, in . . . in some ways I'm a translator between these language games. You know, there is a business language game, financial business game . . . and then there's the IT department who are doing all of the changes, and their particular language game.

As soon as the word 'translator' passes into the conversation it feels right. There is a distinct bodily shift that is more profound in its sense of release than any of the preceding terms. In a stumbling, roundabout, awkward way I have acquired a handle to my felt sense and, as Gendlin (1996) observes, this is frequently the way it is. It is not an emotional response. I am not elated or disappointed in what has transpired. Instead, it is as if something has 'clicked' in much the same way as if, using a sports analogy, I have struck a ball in the middle of the bat. From that point on I felt as if there was no turning back from the insight I had gained. By putting a handle to my felt sense, my understanding of project management practice would never again be the same.

The Competencies of the Virtuoso Project Manager

Despite having achieved a significant personal insight into my understanding of project management practice, the problem of what to do now remained. Whilst I felt my own work would be well served by what my reflections had revealed, the point of my research was to make a broader contribution to project management practice as a whole. Having identified what I felt were the shortcomings of the traditional methods of project management, and recognised what constituted the actual methods of my own practice, I decided to explore whether my experience resonated with the wider project management community.

To this end, I interviewed four fellow project managers, using the same method of focusing that Steven had used to interview me. I chose these four individuals because of their wide experience and the success they had demonstrated in executing corporate sector projects. I had worked with all of them over the years and I knew from personal experience that they held many of the same views on the inadequacy of the traditional project management method in particular, and on project management practice in general. I wanted to see if the idea of project management as 'translating between languages' resonated with them as it had with me.

My purpose in conducting the research was to articulate a more advanced set of project management competencies, one that Cicmil and Hodgson (2006b) describe as expert or 'virtuoso'. The intention was not to replace existing competencies as described by such standards as Prince-2 and the PMBoK. The purpose was to understand their limitations and address their shortcomings in dealing with the complexities and uncertainties of projects in the contemporary corporate environment. In doing so I aimed to describe a set of competencies based on the way virtuoso project managers actually worked on a day-to-day basis.

The Existential Hermeneutic of Redescription

Using the insight of project management as the translation between language games as my organising theme, I conducted an extensive review of the relevant literature. I ultimately settled on the existential hermeneutic method of Richard Rorty as providing the best approach for articulating a virtuoso set of project management competencies. Rorty's pragmatic view of language as 'action-tools for getting what we want' (1990:641) resonated deeply with the understanding I had developed of project management practice. From Rorty's perspective, a specific language is what defines sophisticated human practices. Each language provides definitions of right and wrong behaviour, good and bad outcomes, correct and incorrect procedure etc. Such definitions are, by and large, non-translatable into other languages (i.e. they are incommensurable) (Rorty 1979).

Rorty argues that as a result of a number of historical 'mistakes', the specialist languages that we use today are heavily invested in notions of 'truth' (Rorty 1979:158). Something is good if it is true. Our languages gained this focus, Rorty thinks, during the historical period of the Enlightenment, when scientific discoveries were transforming the way people viewed the world (Rorty 1979). The success of the scientific method in discovering the laws of the natural world in the areas of physics, chemistry and biology, led the intellectuals of the time to believe that the same method could be applied to the human world with equal success. All this led to the creation of 'social' scientific languages such as economics, psychology and anthropology (Flyvbjerg 2001).

The problem, Rorty argues, is that the purpose of social languages differs from scientific ones. The language of science aims at discovering the truths of the natural world, which it attempts to encapsulate in the form of 'laws' such as the law of thermodynamics or the law of gravity. The social sciences attempt to emulate this purpose by seeking the 'truth' of human nature and embodying them in a set of laws (Rorty 1989). Yet, as Peter Watson observes, 'today, two centuries after the end of the Enlightenment, we still can't say for sure what laws human nature obeys or even if these laws are the same as those that obtain in the "hard' sciences"' (2005:744).

The failure of the social sciences to achieve the same success as the natural sciences is, Rorty argues, because social languages are imbued with issues of meaning that constantly exceed the objective facts. It is meaning that separates the social and the scientific. The language of science provides a tool for understanding how the world around us operates, but is far less useful in understanding what that means to us as human beings (Rorty 1989). Social science has therefore largely failed because it has inherited the wrong kind of language. In attempting (and failing) to uncover the truth of human nature, social science has largely ignored the meaning of what it has attempted to describe (Rorty 1999).

It was through reflection on my own practice, and by paying attention to the bodily felt sense of the problems I was experiencing, that I realised the implications of Rorty's thinking for project management. Project management, like other languages such as economics and psychology, is a language that operates in the human domain. Like economics and psychology, it also suffers from an investment in *truth*. The language of project management attempts to provide certainty through the rigorous application of rational, linear techniques (Thomas 2006). As a practice, project management shares the same assumptions of science, insofar as it assumes that a single method can define and resolve a problem under any circumstances, irrespective of context (Cicmil and Hodgson 2006a). The result is a language of project management that is not capable of addressing the *meaning* of the project for the stakeholders. The language of project management seeks to *measure* the project instead.

Rorty's proposal is that languages aimed at addressing the social aspects of the world should abandon notions of truth for notions of 'what works' (Rorty 1979:375). What works in the context of the social are meaningful descriptions. Truth in a social context, Rorty insists, are those descriptions we have settled on *because* they were meaningful, or because they allowed us to lead better lives or, in the case of project management, because they appeared to improve the way we work.

I came to realise that projects were considered successful because they 'worked' and not because they were delivered within the original measurements of time, cost and specification. By and large, provided the stakeholders saw the meaning of the project *realised*, they largely ignored the artificial parameters provided by the traditional project management language. By focusing on managing the *meaning* of the project as opposed to simply *measuring* it, I felt that a project manager could be far more successful in delivering their projects.

Rorty's method for managing the meaning we seek in our social languages is called 'redescription' (Rorty 1979:325). Redescription represents Rorty's particular variation of existential hermeneutics, and is distinguished by an ironic approach to language (Rorty 1989). In the context of project management, an ironic approach means that the project manager does not see any one language in their organisation as invested with more *truth* than any other, including the language of project management. All languages are tools for creating and sharing meaning within and between organisations.

Every specialist practice of the organisation constitutes what Rorty calls a 'language-game' (Rorty 1979:384). The language-game provides the agreed upon conventions of right and wrong or good and bad and invites constructive activity to take place within the confines of the practice. It is between the various practices of the organisation that language-games tend to breakdown as the 'truths' of one practice do not translate easily into the 'truths' of another (Rorty 1989). For any given problem, accountants, financiers, operations, HR etc., will all provide different descriptions that are based in the language of their practice. Each will be correct in terms of their practice, but frequently untranslatable into any other.

Karl Marx (1845) said, 'the philosophers have only interpreted the world, in various ways: the point, however, is to *change* it'. The 'hermeneutic circle' (Heidegger 1966:153) embodies the principle of change with a cycle of practice–reflection–practice. This process allowed for a continual refinement of my understanding as I moved back and forth between my practice and my research to see if the themes resonated with my fellow practitioners. Crucial to a hermeneutic perspective is the role of disruption in generating a reflective stance. The specific form that disruption takes is that of a disruption in meaning in the language games in an organisation. Redescription is the art of seeing disruption in meaning as an opportunity to bring different language-games into conversation with each other for the greater good. Project managers stand at the intersection between numerous language-games in their organisation and, as such, redescription offers a powerful tool to the virtuoso project manager for realising that greater good.

It was, however, a crucial element of the understanding that my research brought about that Rortian 'redescription' was not the final word in project management competency. Nor, indeed, was it the only word. It represented an alternate orientation towards my practice amidst a veritable universe of possibilities. My existential questioning, and the phenomenological investigations that flowed from it, had led me down this particular path and offered myself, and hopefully others, valuable insights into the meaning of project management practice. That, I have come to understand, is the true power of research in the hermeneutic, existential and phenomenological mode: the recognition that from each starting point, and from each and every questioning of one's relationship to their practice, there is an extraordinary range of research avenues to be explored. Such questioning and research never ends, but is a continual interplay between practice and reflection that the dedicated professional will incorporate into the very construct of their profession.

Since the completion of my thesis I have begun working with colleagues, both academics and practitioners, in Australia and overseas to take the general research model outlined above and apply it to other aspects of practice both within project management, and in other professional areas as well. A particular area of research interest is medical practice. Operating as it does between a plethora of languages, medical, legal, scientific, technical and social, the medical practice in the twenty-first century, whether it is a GP or a city hospital, faces unique challenges that my colleagues and I believe hermeneutic research is well placed to help cope with.

Work is currently underway to establish a formal research office dedicated to pursuing research into organisational practices in a hermeneutic, existential and phenomenological mode.

References

Arnold, SJ and Fischer, E, 1994, 'Hermeneutics and consumer research', *Journal of Consumer Research*, 21, June, pp. 55–69.

Bloch, M, Blumberg, S and Laartz, J, 2012, 'Delivering large scale IT projects on time, on budget, and on value', *McKinsey Quarterly*, vol. 27, Fall, available online at: http://www.mckinsey.com/insights/business_technology/delivering_large-scale_it_projects_on_time_on_budget_and_on_value, accessed 1 July 2015.

Cicmil, S and Hodgson, D, 2006a, 'Are projects real? The PMBOK and the legitimation of project management knowledge', in D Hodgson and S Cicmil (eds), *Making projects critical*, Palgrave, Basingstoke, pp. 29–50.

Cicmil, S and Hodgson, D, 2006b, 'New possibilities for project management theory: a critical engagement', *Project Management Journal*, vol. 37, no. 3, pp. 111–22.

Dreyfus, HL, 1991, *Being-in-the-world: A commentary on Heidegger's being and time division 1*, Massachusetts Institute of Technology, Cambridge.

Flyvbjerg, B, 2001, *Making social science matter: Why social inquiry fails and how it can succeed again*, 2nd edn, Cambridge University Press, Cambridge.

Flyvbjerg, B, 2012, 'Why mass media matter and how to work with them: phronesis and mega-projects', in B Flyvberg, T Landman and S Schram (eds), *Real Social Science: Applied Phronesis*, Cambridge University Press, Cambridge, pp. 95–121.

Gendlin, E, 1981, *Focusing*, Bantam Books, New York.

Gendlin, E, 1996, *Focusing-oriented psychotherapy: A manual of the experiential method*, Guilford Press, New York.

Group, TS, 2009, *CHAOS summary report on IT industry projects*, http://www1.standishgroup.com/newsroom/chaos_2009.php%3E, accessed 24 June 2012.

Heidegger, M, 1993, *Martin Heidegger: Basic writings*, Harper Collins, San Francisco.

Heidegger, M, 1996, *Being and time*, SUNY Press, Albany.

MacIntyre, A, 1984, *After virtue – a study in moral theory*, 2nd edn, University of Notre Dame Press, Notre Dame.

Marx, K, 1845, 'Theses of Feuerbach' in K Marx and F Engles, *Marx/Engels selected eorks*, Vol. 1. Progress Publishers, Moscow, pp. 13–15.

PMI, 2013, *A guide to the project management body of knowledge (PMBOK) Fifth Edition*, Project Management Institute, Newtown Square.

Rolfe, B and Segal, S, 2011, 'Opening the Space of Project Management: A Phenomenological Approach', *Philosophy of management*, vol. 10, no. 1, pp. 43–60.

Rorty, R, 1979, *Philosophy and the mirror of nature*, Princeton University Press, Princeton.

Rorty, R, 1989, *Contingency, irony, and solidarity*, Cambridge University Press, Cambridge.

Rorty, R, 1990, 'Truth and freedom: A reply to Thomas McCarthy', *Critical Enquiry*, vol. 16, no. pp. 633–43.

Rorty, R, 1999, *Philosophy and social hope*, Penguin Books, London.

Segal, S, 1999, 'The existential conditions of explicitness: an Heideggerian perspective', *Studies in Continuing Education*, vol. 21, no. 1, pp. 73–89.

Seidman, IE, 1991, *Interviewing as qualitative research: A guide for researchers in education and the social sciences*, Teachers College Press, New York.

Thomas, J, 2006, 'Problematizing project management', in D Hodgson and S Cicmil (eds), *Making projects critical*, Palgrave, Basingstoke, pp. 90–107.

Todres, L, 2007, *Embodied enquiry: Phenomenological touchstones for research, psychotherapy and spirituality*, Palgrave Macmillan, New York.

Todres, L and Galvin, KT, 2008, 'Embodied interpretation: A novel way of evocatively re-presenting meanings in phenomenological research', *Qualitative Research*, vol. 8, no. 5, pp. 568–83.

Watson, P, 2005, *Ideas: A history from fire to Freud*, Orion Books, London.

Chapter 5

Finding My Researcher Voice

From Disorientation to Embodied Practice

Rachelle Arkles

This chapter is an account of how 'being-in-question' in the lived experience of questioning itself changes the shape of research inquiry. 'Being-in-question' elucidates a process for bringing to light the significance that lies beneath the research endeavour. That is, the element that drives a research undertaking forward and gives expression to its practice intentions. My aim in this chapter is to describe and offer some thoughts on the experiential learning that took place, primarily in the first half of a doctoral journey, as a non-Indigenous researcher engaged in a study of experience and meaning in caregiving, ageing and dementia with family members of an older Aboriginal person in urban New South Wales.[1]

The scope of the discussion covers the period of transition where the approach shifts from an envisaged inquiry of dementia perception and caregiver experience to a realisation that the phenomenology I am engaging in is closest to an existential, hermeneutic practice. This is a realisation that comes about in the context of doing the research. Experiencing the research enables a questioning of assumptions about the research thus opening up new ways of being in the research.

I disclose my understanding of this process by drawing on the fieldwork notes that detail the course of my engagement in this community based study of caregivers' experience. I revisit the disruptions, interactions and uncertainties that constitute the 'data' of my own and others' experience. These early

1 The PhD study was a sub-study in the broader *Koori Growing Old Well Study*, Aboriginal Health and Ageing Research Program, Neuroscience Research Australia & University of New South Wales; (NHMRC Project Grant 510347), 2008–2012. I acknowledge with gratitude the financial support for the PhD study provided by the Australian Centre for Population Ageing Research (AIPAR), now known as CEPAR (ARC Centre of Excellence in Population Ageing Research), as well as my supervisory team, Professor Lisa Jackson Pulver, Director of Muru Marri, School of Public Health and Community Medicine (SPHCM) at the University of New South Wales (UNSW); Dr Joanne Travaglia, co-supervisor at SPHCM-UNSW; and Dr Claire Jankelson (Macquarie Graduate School of Management) for her hermeneutic mentorship.

encounters and occurrences become something of a template for the remainder of the research as they signal the significance of the ontological–existential dimension of experience as a way into understanding and interpretation. They allow me to recognise that existential discomfort is an important means for grasping the significance of the phenomenon being researched. Still further, these disruptions become a critical resource for reframing the phenomenon under inquiry.

The Phenomenological Framework

The conceptual framework for this chapter derives from existential, hermeneutic phenomenology, which Todres and Wheeler, describe as 'natural bedfellows' (2001, p. 6). The emphasis here is less on hermeneutic phenomenology as a philosophy and methodology and more on its living expression as a mode of research practice. I work with the 'complementary' elements Todres and Wheeler (2001, p. 2) refer to in 'grounding' a phenomenological study of the dementia experience in the lived world of Aboriginal caregivers; in making sense of my researcher 'positioning'; and in drawing from my situated embodiment in a 'language of existential experiencing' to disclose the world of the research relation.

I draw from two seminal ideas in Martin Heidegger's, *Being and Time* (1962). The first is that in a medicalised (now bio-technological) world it is easy to overlook the significance of the meaning of 'Being'. The second idea is the notion that 'Being is not Presence' (Harman 2007, p. 1). The impact of these two influential ideas for experience driven research is two-fold. The first rejects the notion of subject–object duality, that is, the view that a thinking subject exists in a separate domain in a world which is the object of its intentional thought. On the contrary, Heidegger's notion of 'being-in-the-world' discloses our relationship to the world in which we live and as such can never be the 'object' of our thought, but rather, emerges imperceptibly from a background of 'intelligibility' (what we might understand as our socio-cultural inheritance) into thought.

The second, namely, the notion that 'Being is not Presence' invites us to reflect on the idea of ourselves as a 'concealed presence' as we go about our daily business. This draws attention to two planes of inquiry in human science research: a realm that is visible (present and tangible) and one that is invisible (liminal and elusive). This is a conception that complicates the notion of 'truth' beyond measurable, observable entities. It demands we think about what kind of 'truth' this is and in what ways this can be demonstrated, both as a mode of reasoning and in the display of research as 'findings'.

Further, the idea of concealment contained in the notion that 'Being is not Presence' reveals a space of tension for the conduct of research in a contemporary world. In a post-colonial and intercultural environment the phenomenological researcher must navigate between the universal structure of human experiencing (Heidegger's philosophy of 'being-in-the-world') and the 'situatedness' of a particular historical embodiment (Sartre's existentialist thought) (Dreyfus and Wrathall 2005). In the former, the locus for researcher reflexivity is to bring to the surface the fundamental obscurity characterising 'everyday' or habitual practice. In the latter, the researcher comes face to face with Sartre's notion of 'bad faith', an idea which existential scholars of race describe as a phenomenon of 'not admitting what I see, what I do, or where I supposedly stand' (Gordon 1995, p. 16).

The process of critical sense-making occurs through the practice of reflexivity which is 'foundational' to the hermeneutic phenomenological tradition (Walsh 2003). In Heidegger's hermeneutics it is encapsulated by the concept of the hermeneutic circle: a process of sense-making embedding constituent parts into a whole through their referential meaning in relation to each other and to a totality of meaning. We are, according to Heidegger, part of, and not outside of, the hermeneutic circle of understanding.

Building on Heidegger, Gadamer's hermeneutics views reflexivity as a 'fusion of researcher and participant horizons' through the ontological nature of language as social relation (Moran 2000). The significance of language in this conception is that in it we see disclosed a certain way of 'being-in-the-world' and that it is through language that we come to comprehend something about the nature of that existence.

In a more critical hermeneutic application, Ricoeur's idea of 'the long hermeneutic detour' extends hermeneutic phenomenology's relevance to issues of political alterity and the redress of social and civic injustice (Kearney 1996). Yet, it does so in a way that foregrounds the temporal, historicised nature of our existence by shining a light on how time and history express themselves in our experiencing (Kemp and Rasmussen 1989).

As will become evident throughout this chapter, this perspective resonates powerfully for this research as it highlights the entanglement of the individual story within a wider historical narrative. Caregivers in an Aboriginal 'world' of ageing and dementia are in this sense both people and a People. What is more, in 'shared history' there is the entanglement of the researcher's narrative (my narrative) with those with whom research is conducted (Jones and Jenkins 2008).

These differing accounts of reflexivity provide a scholarly language for capturing the 'lived experience' at the core of the research endeavour. Yet, it is the living experience of research practice that brings these hermeneutic conceptions to life. In this regard, Gendlin's (1962) notion of 'implicit experience' offers a way into researcher sense-making through his concept of 'felt experience' which, he argues, operates at a different level from a process of objective reasoning or logic. This experiential, even pre-conceptual dimension of experience becomes an important source of 'data' for analysis and a meaningful resource for researcher sense-making.

The Emerging Visibility of the Study's Research Question

The study sets out to learn about the experience and meaning of 'dementia' for family caregivers of an older Aboriginal person. The purpose for doing so is to contribute to the knowledge required for service provision in an area of growing public health concern. While dementia has emerged as a global phenomenon it is predominantly described in the literature in 'Western diagnostic' terms (Mackenzie et al. 2006). Much of the cross-cultural literature, including amongst Indigenous populations, illustrates the ways in which dementia perception differs across cultural environments, including that it may not be recognised as an illness (Arkles et al. 2010).

Yet, there is a paucity of information about the experience of family carers, particularly for Aboriginal families living in urban areas. I can only speculate as to how 'dementia' – as a global phenomenon of population ageing – is 'held' by families within the communities that I am engaging with. I wonder how 'dementia' makes its appearance in day to day living; how and when it becomes visible and recognisable as something other than 'normal ageing'; and in what ways the actions taken by family members arise from the meaningful horizon of their experience. Similarly, I wonder how the interpretations of researchers themselves shape the ways in which dementia in the Aboriginal population is presented in the public domain.

My position as a doctoral researcher with a phenomenological orientation within a broader population based study affords me a unique vantage point. The location of the sub-study (caregivers' experience) within the larger population study (prevalence and risk factors for dementia) places the two studies in relief, highlighting that which is foregrounded and backgrounded in importance to achieve the objectives of the respective studies. I am able to experience from the inside the differences between researching in the interpretive mode (the doctoral study) while being a close observer to research in a more positivist mode (the population study). In both these modes, we as researchers have an embodied relationship to our inquiry and a sensitivity to the importance of relationship building and appropriate cultural protocols for ethical practice in the context of community based research with Aboriginal communities.

There is, however, a distinguishing feature in these respective modes of research practice. In the population study, there is careful monitoring of the researcher's place within the researcher–participant encounter with the aim being impartiality of the research methods. Ambiguities, contingencies and uncertainties are placed aside in the interests of the imperatives of standardisation and comparison as a core feature of the epidemiological requirement. By contrast, in the hermeneutic study, I intentionally enter into the corporeal space of the interview encounter as a resource for knowing.

I engage with moods of disruption and disorientation (both my own and those of participants) as a means of questioning the concepts I bring into the study. The existential discomfort of moods, anxieties, disruptions and 'felt experience' is a portal for opening up to experience, that is, to opening up to the phenomenon of inquiry itself.

Description of the Research Dilemma

When I embark on the study the research question I pose asks, 'what is the experience and meaning of "dementia" for urban family members caring for an older Aboriginal person?' I am drawn to the research question by the promise of its narrative nature, its contextually grounded inquiry and its potential for expanding the interpretive horizons of non-Indigenous researchers (such as myself) and service providers. I conceptualise my empirical research as a telling of experience and action around 'dementia'; how it appears in peoples' lives and how it is lived. My exploratory readings into researching 'lived experience' lead me to phenomenology and hermeneutics, both as philosophical frameworks for understanding and as methodologies for deepening knowledge of the social world (Crotty 1998; Polkinghorne 1988; Van Manen 1990).

While this gives me the direction on paper to proceed, I am mired in a struggle to reconcile the dimensions of my own standpoint in relation to the proposed research with Aboriginal family caregivers. I begin to feel uneasy as a non-Indigenous person basing my inquiry around Aboriginal peoples' experience and meaning. I am mindful of the political complexities of being a 'priority target population' for research purposes. While there is an 'equity' component to this (most notably expressed in the 'Close the Gap Campaign'), it is also a designation that is contested in existential, cultural and representational dimensions (Gordon 2000; Grossman 2003). As Gordon (2000) asks, 'what does it mean to be an 'Other', where 'Other' is characterised as 'a problem to be solved'.[2] Furthermore, I grapple with the notion of a scholarship that lays claim to 'knowing' the experience and meaning of others. How is it possible to step outside of one's perceptual frame?

In this dilemma my gaze is turned towards a reflexive questioning: Who am I? How am I to proceed with this inquiry? In the Aboriginal communities in which I conduct this research there are ongoing reverberations of Australia's colonial history with its legacy of racist policies and practices. In this context how we are with each other in the research relation is

2 'What does it mean to be a problem?' is the title of Chapter 4 in Gordon's book, *Existentia Africana*, Op. cit.

a significant matter. This disrupts and challenges my research stance and practice in a number of ways.

First, there is the problematic concerning how we make meaning of experience that comes from inhabiting 'particular kinds of bodies' (Murphy 2008). During the course of the study I am often asked, 'how is the experience of dementia different for Aboriginal people?' Furthermore, as a non-Aboriginal researcher what do I 'see' in my research with Aboriginal people? This encapsulates a second dilemma, which concerns how it is possible to move beyond the representations we make of each other across cultural, historical and experiential divides. Finally, there is a third point of tension to navigate in this research, namely, between the communal voice (community and organisational stakeholders) and the voice of diverse individuals in a face to face research encounter. This raises the question of how to honour the individual story within the broader public and historical narrative.

The conventions of research practice often struggle to deal with such real life complexity or to cross paradigmatic boundaries of understanding. Yet, it is in the immersion of complexity with all its convolutedness that provides a new experience. We begin to make sense of this experience by entering into a tangible, embodied relation. As Segal writes, 'in order to complete our work, to become attuned, we need to be existentially there' (1998, p. 276). In so doing, the researcher takes the risk of entering into the 'strangeness' of their own 'being' when they begin to see themselves and their practices through the eyes of 'the other'. By 'being-in' complexity and difference that which is to be understood in the understanding of the question starts to uncover itself (Ree 1999). As Ree proclaims, it is the place where 'we stand', 'in relation to the meaning of being in the question' (1999, p. 8), that invites the deepest learning to take place.

This is the central idea of this chapter. How does this ontological understanding become the vehicle for learning from within the practice of our research? What kind of knowing is this? What do we draw from to put into practice this kind of knowledge? Where is the disruption in the research located? These are the kinds of questions that I keep in mind as I conduct the research. This allows for recognition that questions of 'who' and 'how' we are in the research relation constitute a distinctive mode of reflexive practice for social research. It brings the researcher closer to a mode of reflexivity that draws from an ontological–existential dimension of experience with all its contradictions, uncertainties and opportunities for greater attunement rather than from an epistemological tradition in which a version of the world is imparted to us in hypothetical or theoretical form.

In the following section of this chapter, I provide an account of being in a complex and contested research environment. This raises a number of questions illuminating the practice of the research.

Entering into Research: From Expectation to Dwelling in Disorientation

What is the Research Story?

I begin the study with the understanding that it is about the experience of dementia for caregivers of an older, Aboriginal person. As I alluded to earlier, this research question arises as a 'knowledge gap' identified in a literature review preceding the start of this inquiry, showing little information about Aboriginal families' experience of dementia (Arkles et al. 2010). At a pragmatic level, the usefulness of asking this question is that it seeks to produce the kind of 'data' relevant to the needs of families seeking dementia information, services and support.

At a paradigmatic level however, the question arises from a belief in the capacity of research to 'find' tangible truths that can be translated into policy and service outcomes. I am periodically asked, 'So what are you finding about Indigenous people and dementia?' I struggle to find a sound bite for this question about the dementia experience. It is a complex, often hidden, and long story, and its significance only becomes apparent as the research proceeds.

What is the Phenomenon Being Researched?

The phenomenon I am seeking to understand is 'dementia' in an Aboriginal community context. Potential study participants, that is, family carers of frail older people fall into three broad categories: those whose older relative is showing signs of cognitive decline but who still maintain an active community life; those whose relative is frail and incapacitated and, as with the first group, have not had a medical diagnosis of dementia; and a third group whose older family member is at home or in a nursing home with a medical diagnosis of mid to end-stage dementia.

Most of the families in the first two groupings, I am told, 'are not willing to address a diagnosis of dementia'. This suggests the concept of denial, a perspective that has meaning in the referential world of the medical diagnosis but which cannot be assumed in the referential world of family life. I attempt to peel away the Western diagnosis of 'dementia' and 'denial' by wondering what it is that the family see. I accompany a community health worker on her visit to an older lady to gain a better feel.

> The lady lives alone but her unit is surrounded by neighbours who keep an eye out for her. There is disagreement in her family as to whether she has dementia or not and this causes friction and upset. When we arrive, the kettle is on the boil and we join the lady and her neighbour for tea. She moves around her space slowly. She is a little confused with

her pills. After an explanation, the community worker is reassured that her medication regimen is under control. We settle down with our tea. The older lady tells us stories of her engagement in her community. She is animated and her commitment and enjoyment of community life is deeply sustaining.

I come away from this visit with the feel of something quite ambiguous. Is this 'dementia' I am seeing? Is this the space between the meaning of a diagnostic label 'dementia' and the meaning of it as a living experience? Either way, as a hermeneutic researcher I must deal with the comprehension of an uncertain phenomenon.

What is Culture?

While getting to know the communities I will be conducting my research in, I work on the pilot study for the main population survey. The questionnaire is long and detailed, comprised mainly of closed questions and Likert scales (an approach for scaling responses in a question). I interview a woman who has volunteered her time for the pilot study. In one section questions are asked about 'Aboriginal languages spoken' and 'identification with tribal grouping' as markers of cultural affiliation. These are standardised questions drawn from commonly used Indigenous population surveys. The woman being interviewed answers that she is not identified with any 'tribal, traditional or clan group' nor 'speaks any Aboriginal language'. I tick the boxes. After a pause she speaks. 'Growing up on the mission, we weren't allowed any of this. You would be punished for speaking your language'. Then there is silence.

I soon realise that what this lady is describing is a profoundly cultural experience: that of growing up as an Aboriginal person on a mission within a colonial regime of control through assimilation. Yet, I wonder how this standardised marker of 'connection to culture' will be interpreted by readers unfamiliar with these localised political and social histories. It brings to mind the argument of the social researcher, Mishler, regarding the importance of context in narrative understanding without which survey responses suffer a 'disconnection from their socio-cultural ground of meaning' (Mishler 1986, p. 23). In other words, instead of assuming a notion of 'culture', or its lack thereof, the contextualisation of culture invites a questioning of 'what the culture in question is' (Waldram 2006, p. 72).

What is a Subject?

Two years into my doctorate, I am struggling to obtain the number of participants initially envisaged for the study. I am in contact with numerous potential participants and am working through the requisite community networks. People are in crisis. Families are in crisis. There are strokes, hospitalisations, daily coping with the needs of frail elders. There are those looking after relatives with 'difficult behaviours' who await diagnosis or respite care. There are those who do not wish to get involved. There are others who express a reluctance to talk about painful issues. There are those who've agreed and then subsequently can't be contacted. There are caregivers who themselves are unwell. Others work long days and come home to multiple family responsibilities. In some cases, the elder person has now passed.

As I wait for more respondents, I start to pause, slow down and close in. I recognise a certain parallel experience described to me by a respondent as her world contracted to accommodate her mother's illness. I struggle against this feeling of 'being-slow' in my body. *I'm a researcher; I need to stay on track. What must I do to proceed?*

Still, I am deeply immersed in this experiential space. The community is starting to take on a tangible, living presence. My telephone exchanges with potential respondents are both revealing and concealing of a complex reality. *When, and in what situations, is it appropriate to approach families in crisis to take part in research? Where might the problem for families be located? Am I prepared for the depth and pain of what I am about to hear?*

In this space of questioning the notion of 'a research subject' is starting to look in and of itself like a limited and incomplete research entity. The subject I am now seeing is expanding into a palpable, complex research space. Without explicitly realising it, I am entering into what Heidegger conceptualises as the 'context of concern'. That is, the manner in which we live or 'dwell' in a set of concerns. This appreciation moves me closer to the idea of the referential whole, whereby I begin to grasp the significance of the research as a totality of meaning rather than as a series of interrelated components. This is not the understanding I started out with.

Whose Experience and Meaning is This?

At the start of my study I reflect on the elders in my own family to search for any personal experience with dementia. I am not aware that I have ever personally encountered it. After listening to a participant's bewildered account of seeing her parent in a nursing home, I found a memory that I had not thought about for decades. It concerned my grandmother who at the time was in her mid-eighties and living in a residential nursing home. I recall what happened on one of my visits:

> I found her seated on the edge of her bedside chair. The others were lying in their beds. As I came into my grandmother's line of vision, she lurched towards me. Her eyes were magnified through her large spectacles and her demeanour was agitated. She started speaking in a language I did not understand. It was the vernacular of her mother tongue from the other side of the world. I was startled by this outpouring.

She grabbed my arms tightly and urged me in this foreign language and snatches of English, 'Hurry . . . Leave . . . Police . . . Police coming . . . Hurry home'. I tried to reassure her but it was to no avail. I left feeling unsettled and disoriented.

The memory recalled elicits a 'felt sense' of 'dementia', something I have not been aware of within the experience of my own family. Yet, through the research encounter my own 'world' is beginning to uncover itself. The research question is starting to 'inhabit me', a phenomenon described by Van Manen (1990) as the hallmark of phenomenological questioning.

What Do I 'See' in Research with Aboriginal People?

On one of my first visits into a local community I am introduced to a prominent community figure *as a researcher*. As we shake hands his voice is playful but he asks me, '*You're not an anthropologist are you?*' Before I have time to respond he continues, '*They think they know us and can write about us. But we know better. We tell them whatever they want to hear! They don't actually know us.*'

The significance of this encounter is that it illuminates a deeply held suspicion by many Indigenous communities when confronted with Western research and researchers. It arises from Australia's colonial legacy and the ways in which Aboriginal people and communities have been manipulated (and in some cases harmed) in the service of colonial or 'White' research interests (Anderson 2007; Smith 1999). Discomforting as this encounter is, it is instructive in my learning. It presents me with the opportunity to 'dig deep' into my embodied discomfort as a 'White' researcher undertaking research in an Indigenous space and to ask myself difficult questions about whose interests are being served in the conduct of the research.

In Heideggerian terms it has thrown my 'being' into question. '*Who am I and where am I located in this inquiry?*' I am reminded of Lewis Gordon's (2000) provocative question for human science researchers, namely, 'is it possible to study a racial formation as a human formation?' In this highly charged research space I think about what it means to encounter an (Other).

Being-in Question and Entering Unfamiliar Ground

In the encounters described above, I enter into a series of calibrated existential states. I am 'in confusion', 'in disruption', 'in uncertainty', 'in disorientation', 'in bewilderment' and 'in discomfort'. I am losing hold of the coherence and purpose of my original research question. In fact, far from the purposeful demeanour of the research 'scientist', I am 'dwelling' in a state of existential concern. In the language of Heidegger, I am in a state of anxiety, an uncertainty in which the foundations of my practice have been taken away.

Paradoxically for Heidegger, anxiety is also a state of care, in that it is in this state that we 'dwell' in a set of concerns. It matters to me that things are not what they seem. In this stance, the world appears complex, contradictory and capable of many meanings. How does this perspective fit with what Heidegger calls the 'average everydayness' of being a researcher?

While I embark on the study contemplating the perceptions and experiences of Aboriginal families dealing with the 'dementia' phenomenon, it is my own researcher experience and perception that I am grappling with. The research question as I originally formulate it speaks to the 'pre-reflective state of my familiarity' that Heidegger refers to, as I have not yet entered into a questioning mode on the question itself. This arises because in the 'average everydayness' of my practice as a researcher, I am oriented towards finding, and drawing from information about tangible, visible entities. How then do I proceed when nothing tangible seems to be happening; when the phenomenon I am researching is elusive and un-named; when I start to sense the presence of something significant but don't yet have a scholarly language to give it legitimacy; and when I am in a state of disorientation, discomfort and unknowing?

Entering in: From Disorientation to Reframing

In their chapter on 'weaving a phenomenological text', Jones and Borbasi (2003) talk about the point at which one is ready to 'commit an account to paper'. This is the point at which they write, 'One has made enough sense of the data to render any account at all' (2003, p. 93). This point occurs for me as early as my initial encounter with the first of the study's participants. I experience a strong sense that something significant and distinctive is characterising this research. I recall writing in my fieldwork notes after this first interview that '*I was reeling*' from the raw power of the telling and that I had been unsettled by what had been revealed. Then a similar thing happened with the second participant. In both these interviews, I bear witness to a powerful existential struggle. It surfaces repeatedly throughout the interview in oft repeated phrases and in the emotionality of its telling. The telling moves backwards and forwards in time and place, taking both me and participants to a depth of conversation I could not have anticipated at the start of the inquiry. I have entered into peoples' lives at a time of profound ontological–existential pain and this places me into these stories in a powerful way. I feel bound to bring something of this quality to light in the textual display of the research.

These first interview encounters become something of a template for the remainder of the study. What is emerging are two interrelated yet distinctive domains of the experience of caring. At one level, there are accounts of caregiving in descriptions of what is involved in providing daily assistance, what happens and when. The other level is coming from a different plane of experience; a place largely hidden from view. These struggles are told in a circuitous movement of past, present and future. Their purpose goes beyond that of 'satisfaction' with the care provided or the 'nuts' and 'bolts' of caregiving itself. They seem to be reaching for a resolution where the caregiving situation being lived with can be made sense of in a wider field of temporal–emotional significance.

I recognise early on that I am dealing with a particular kind of 'story' or narrative. Glen Martin talks about stories 'as acts of self-disclosure', in which something about the central character is revealed: who they are as a person and where is their struggle (Martin 2011, p. 19). This quality is in the forefront of participant telling. It also speaks to the moods of my own uncertainty and disruption, and in so doing alerts me to the significance of the grappling underlying the practice of the research.

In the presuppositions contained in the study's original research question, I enter into moods of disorientation, disruption and existential struggle. These moods disrupt the way I exist as a researcher in the world. In stepping outside habitual research practices, I allow for other learnings to be revealed. I refocus the research question to accommodate the complexities of 'being-in research' in a discomforting and uncertain space. In this process, the inquiry shifts from a study of other peoples' caregiving experiences to what it means to be immersed in a set of existential concerns in the research relation itself.

Meaning Making in the Interview Encounter: From Reframing to Embodied Practice

The idea of the formality of the research encounter is in my mind as the place where one 'gathers data'. As it happens, I am privy to a much closer world of experiencing in this community based research. I drop people here and there as I live and work close by. We take extra underwear to an elderly mother in hospital. We pick up relatives. We talk in the car and over a coffee. I drop in on a group that is a significant support in a respondent's life. She wants me to see something they are making there. We chat together. I talk about my background, heritage and grandparents. 'Now you are sharing your stories with us', my respondent quips, and I glimpse myself now from the gaze of the researched.

The 'substantive interview' too takes place in real life and real time, mostly in respondents' homes. Family members drop in, the telephone rings, we make tea. We talk. Conversation enters into these informal spaces between 'normal living' and the 'professional interview', the latter being a zone where consent forms are signed and I set out with an interview guide. I pivot around the respondent's narrative. I try to think where I am placed in this research relation and what the nature of the boundary is between us (Fine 1994). Yet, 'research', by that I mean the generation of something new *is* happening in this 'between' space. As the writer, Siri Hustvedt, observes of 'the space between the analyst and the analysand', it is a place where 'emotional truths are brought to light and narratives remade' (Hustvedt 2012, p. 159).

The narratives of our interview contain the moods of disruption, despair, dread and hope as family members face the decline and impending death of their loved ones. I immerse myself in these storied accounts. In one, Doreen[3] describes the first time she saw her mother in a nursing home (my account is in italics).

> Well, when I came through the lift all I could see was mum sitting at the table and it was her back . . . I don't know what it was that I'd seen but . . . I didn't like it. I did not like the place and I went in and I signed some papers and I came back out and I just don't know . . . I couldn't sleep and the next morning I rang them up and I said, 'I'm coming to get mum'.

The phrase 'seen from the back' jolts me into my own disorientation. I recognise my own experiencing with my grandmother in this description. I can see so clearly the narrow slump of my grandmother's frail shoulders; her thinning grey hair, from the back, as I saw her in that place, the nursing home. She could be, as Doreen says, 'any poor old lady in that place', not *my* grandmother. I am moved to speak.

> *She doesn't have a story in that place*, I murmur. No they don't. And like with mum and her culture, they probably don't understand . . . *what aspects are you thinking of?* Well, what I mean is . . . how she feels inside herself, in her heart and in her soul and in her whole body about who she is and where she comes from and all the things that's happened in her life . . . How are they going to notice when she doesn't respond? Are they just going to think that it's normal; just an old woman that got dementia and all the things that are different to what we know?

Our conversation continues and moves into a deeper level of exchange. Sometimes we just sit with this sadness. We seem to be segueing into each other's stories and at one point I'm not sure where my story with my grandmother ends and Doreen and her mother's continues. What I do know is that this is how I came to 'see' my grandmother's 'dementia', and as with Doreen's mother, this was the first time it was named.

'Entering-into-experience' is entering into a specific form of embodied awareness as a resource for knowing the world. This form of sense-making is, as Todres describes, 'an authenticating or validating procedure arising from the participation of the lived body rather than from a person's cognitive

---

3 A fictional name.

processes' (Todres 2007, p. 31). In the living space of the interview encounter, we find the words that give expression to our discomfort. It is a truth arising from the living space between us. Doreen's use of the phrase, 'when I saw her from the back', and my use of the phrase, 'she had no story in that place', struck a deep chord and brought the 'truth' of both our experiencing into view. Prior to this Doreen was compelled to act on her 'felt sense' by removing her mother from the nursing home, despite having no words to explain why. For my own part, it was the trigger to ask troubling questions about the presence of 'dementia' in my own family, despite this never being named.

Through the dialogical encounter something significant comes to be disclosed illustrating Gadamer's conceptualisation of language 'as the medium in which understanding is realised' (Moran 2000, pp. 248–9). It also brings home how the 'objective' dimension of experience is not the same as its 'lived' dimension.

The Significance of Ontological Reflexivity for Disclosing the World of the Research Relation

I have arrived at the core business of the research endeavour: how to disclose the 'world' of dementia for Aboriginal family caregivers, and in so doing, disclose my own world as a researcher in the world. The question of what it means to be a caregiver, and what it means to be a researcher, arises from that place of disruption where we 'dwell in a set of concerns' in the caregiving and research relation respectively. My struggles to articulate the relevance of the inquiry within a post-colonial research space have seen me grappling with how the concept of reflexivity in hermeneutic phenomenology is distinctive and useful when looked at in conversation with other forms of reflexivity common to contemporary scholarship.

In this dynamic, what is revealed is a hermeneutic process as engagement in the research moves backwards and forwards in a manifold dialogue: first, between my experiencing as researcher and the discourse of scholarly texts. Here, one enters into the scholarship in a process akin to the movement of a hermeneutic circle in the quest to continually deepen one's questioning (Boell and Cecez-Kecmanovic 2010). It is a synergistic movement between one's experiencing in the research practice and the language of scholarly texts.

Second, I enter into a reflexive conversation between the 'data' of my own experiencing and the 'data' of participant experience in the existential space of the research relation. In this 'between' space one draws from immersion in an embodied situation. 'Being-there' is therefore descriptive of a quality of immersion as opposed to an account of the nature of 'entities', as Kompridis describes, 'how one's experience is, "prefigures" the process of how one comes to understand that experience' (Kompridis 2006, p. 33). This immersion in the situation is a 'dwelling in a set of concerns', which in

Heidegger's ontology begins its reflexive impulse from within a referential field of everyday living and comprehension. In the anxieties, disruptions and disorientations that arise in the space 'between' the researcher and participants, one finds oneself navigating between that which is familiar to one's practice and that which is strange to one's practice. In the state of estrangement from one's habitual or 'ordinary everyday practice', the disorientation leads the researcher closer towards the significance of what is actually emerging from the lived relation of that practice.

Finally, I reflect on the temporal, historical significance of 'the entanglement of an individual story and its wider historical narrative' (Mankowski and Rappaport 2000), in reaching for the situated research story that is unfolding. This process of 'unconcealment', which is also how 'a world' becomes visible to us, emanates from an ontological field of existence, including the manner in which language and culture are constitutive of 'being' in the sense outlined by Heidegger and Gadamer.

How we exist in the world and in relationship to one another, therefore, can be contrasted with the kinds of 'epistemological arguments', theories and models that underpin a technical discourse (Taylor 1995). For contained in our ontological field of existence, we exist not just as individuals 'in time', but as the embodiment of time, in that we are bearers of a past and a cultural and historical experiencing that projects itself into the future. The significance of this human experience of time, according to the French hermeneutic phenomenologist Paul Ricoeur, is best revealed in narrative form with 'temporality and narrativity being closely related' (Ricoeur, 1980, p. 169). This speaks to the enmeshment between our temporal 'being' and our historical, cultural 'belonging', a concept that is ever present in the narrative of this study, and which I disclose through the study's narrative accounts: my own and that of participants.

In the existential, hermeneutic and phenomenological approach to the practice of my research, I open a space for a different type of learning to take place. Ann Holroyd captures this process when she writes:

> Experience, when approached from a stance of openness, places our mental and intellectual processes at stake, and demonstrates a willingness to surrender our attachments to our current knowledge. Through this way of being, individuals are intent not on knowing more but on knowing differently.
>
> (Holroyd 2007, p. 3 of 12)

In the experience of researching 'dementia' in an Indigenous non-Indigenous research space, I have entered into the learning in a different way to my usual research approaches. I 'go with' the disorientation, anxiety and disruption, recalibrating and reframing my research questioning along the way. The Aboriginal writer, Alexis Wright (2006, p. 3), captures this quality in her tale of communities in the Gulf Country of Australia when she writes, 'It takes a certain kind of knowledge to go with the river. Whatever its mood.'

These are the 'moods' that in Heideggerian language bring the 'context of concern' to visibility. The practical significance of this approach for future research inquiry is that it offers a way of working from inside areas of difference, contention and uncertainty in a variety of professional environments. This has applied relevance for areas of endeavour that cut across diverse experiential or cultural worlds in a global, intercultural and inequitable world. It brings the relational, concealed and holistic dimensions of research practice into visibility thereby challenging research professionals to reveal what is really at stake in their understanding of the research purpose. Reconfiguring understanding through immersion in the world of our research is a core part of this challenge.

References

Anderson, W, 2007, 'The colonial medicine of settler states: comparing histories of indigenous health', *Health and History*, vol. 9, no. 2, pp. 144–154.

Arkles, R, Jackson Pulver, L, Robertson, H, Draper, B, Chalkley, S and Broe, GA, 2010, *Ageing, cognition and dementia in Australian Aboriginal and Torres Strait Islander peoples*, Neuroscience Research Australia and Muru Marri Indigenous Health Unit, University of New South Wales.

Boell, SK and Cecez-Kecmanovic, D, 2010, 'Literature reviews and the hermeneutic circle', *Australian Academic and Research Libraries*, vol. 41, no. 2, pp. 129–144.

Crotty, M, 1998, *The foundations of social research*, Allen and Unwin, Crows Nest, NSW.

Dreyfus, H and Wrathall, MA (eds), 2005, *A companion to Heidegger*, Blackwell Publishing Ltd, Oxford.

Fine, M, 1994, 'Working the hyphens: reinventing self and other in qualitative research', in *Handbook of qualitative research*, eds NK Denzin and YS Lincoln, Sage, Thousand Oaks, CA, pp. 70–82.

Gendlin, ET, 1962, *Experiencing and the creation of meaning. A philosophical and psychological approach to the subjective*, Free Press of Glencoe, New York.

Gordon, LR, 1995, *Fanon and the crisis of European man: an essay on philosophy and the human sciences*, Routledge, New York.

Gordon, LR, 2000, *Existentia Africana*, Routledge, New York, London.

Grossman, M (ed.), 2003, *Blacklines: contemporary critical writing by Indigenous Australians*, Melbourne University Press, Melbourne.

Harman, G, 2007, *Heidegger explained: from phenomenon to thing*, Open Court, Chicago & La Sal, IL.

Heidegger, M, 1962, *Being and time*, Blackwell, Oxford.

Holroyd, AE, 2007, 'Interpretive hermeneutic phenomenology: clarifying understanding', *Indo-Pacific Journal of Phenomenology*, vol. 7, no. 2.

Hustvedt, S, 2012, *Living, thinking, looking*, Hodder and Stoughton, London.

Jones, J and Borbasi, S, 2003, 'Interpretive research: weaving a phenomenological text', in *Writing research: transforming data into text*, eds J Clare & H Hamilton, Churchill Livingstone, Elsevier Science Limited, Edinburgh, pp. 85–101.

Jones, A and Jenkins, K 2008, 'Rethinking collaboration: working the indigene-colonizer hyphen', in *Handbook of Critical and Indigenous Methodologies*, eds NK Denzin, YS Lincoln and LT Smith, SAGE Publications, Thousand Oaks, CA, pp. 471–486.

Kearney, R (ed.), 1996, *Paul Ricoeur: the hermeneutics of action*, SAGE Publications, London, Thousand Oaks, New Delhi.

Kemp, PT and Rasmussen, D (eds) 1989, *The narrative path: the later works of Paul Ricoeur*, The MIT Press, Cambridge, MA, London, England.

Kompridis, N, 2006, *Critique and disclosure*, The MIT Press, Cambridge, MA, London, England.

Mackenzie, J, Bartlett, R and Downs, M, 2006, 'Moving towards culturally competent dementia care: have we been barking up the wrong tree?' *Reviews in Clinical Gerontology*, vol. 15, no. 1, pp. 39–46.

Mankowski, ES and Rappaport, J, 2000, 'Narrative concepts and analysis in spiritually-based communities', *Journal of Community Psychology*, vol. 28, no. 5, pp. 479–493.

Martin, G, 2011, 'The role of stories in the development of values and wisdom as expressions of spirituality', *Journal of Spirituality, Leadership and Management*, vol. 5, no. 1, pp. 14–24.

Mishler, EG, 1986, *Research interviewing: context and narrative*, Harvard University Press, Cambridge, MA, London, England.

Moran, D, 2000, *Introduction to phenomenology*, Routledge, London, New York.

Murphy, A, 2008, 'Feminism and race theory', in *Merleau-Ponty Key Concepts,* eds R Diprose and J Reynolds, Acumen, Stocksfield, UK, pp. 197–206.

Polkinghorne, D, 1988, *Narrative knowing and the human sciences*, SUNY Press, Albany, NY.

Ree, J, 1999, *Heidegger (The Great Philosophers)*, Routledge Chapman and Hall, London, New York.

Ricoeur, P, 1980, 'Narrative time', *Critical Inquiry*, vol. 7, no. 1, pp. 169–190.

Segal, S, 1998, 'The anxiety of strangers and the fear of enemies studies' *Philosophy and Education*, vol. 17, no. 4, pp. 271–282.

Smith, LH, 1999, *Decolonizing methodologies: research and indigenous peoples*, University of Otago Press, Dunedin, New Zealand.

Taylor, C, 1995, *Philosophical arguments*, Harvard University Press, Cambridge, MA, London.

Todres, L, 2007, *Embodied enquiry: phenomenological touchstones for research, psychotherapy and spirituality*, Palgrave Macmillan, Basingstoke, New York.

Todres, L and Wheeler, S, 2001, 'The complementarity of phenomenology, hermeneutics and existentialism as a philosophical perspective for nursing research', *International Journal of Nursing Studies*, vol. 38, no. 1, pp. 1–8.

Van Manen, M, 1990. *Researching lived experience*. The State University of New York Press, Albany, NY.

Waldram, JB, 2006, 'The view from the Hogan: cultural epidemiology and the return to ethnography', *Transcultural Psychiatry*, vol. 43, no. 1, pp. 72–85.

Walsh, R, 2003, 'The methods of reflexivity', *The Humanist Psychologist*, vol. 31, no. 4, pp. 51–66.

Wright, A, 2006, *Carpentaria*, Giramondo Publishing, Artarmon, NSW.

Chapter 6

Being-in-Practice

Making the Leap from the Instrumental Technocratic to an Existential Hermeneutic Practice in Family Business Succession Consulting

Bill Hovey[1,2]

Jean-Paul Sartre (1938, 2010) described the existential anxiety that accompanies making a decision: "There is even a moment right at the start where you have to jump across an abyss: if you think about it you don't do it."

In thinking about their succession, many owners baulk, like Sartre, at jumping the abyss. Instead, they remain fixed: on the edge, locked into a succession dilemma. This chapter describes that dilemma and the evolution of my methodologies and conventions of practice in working with that dilemma.

This evolution underscores my journey from the experience of succession to a theory of succession. It follows Aristotle's (1975) argument that learning *for* practice derives from experience *in* practice. My emergent theory does not offer an alternative to existing theory. Rather, it accommodates the existing whilst offering a way in which it can be expanded – even enhanced.

This chapter is divided into six parts:

The first part describes my lived experience as a succession practitioner. My life-world of succession practice is characterized by the conventions of practice of the extant instrumental technocratic models. I describe frustrations with those models, and the reasons for searching for a new mode of practice.

The next part explores succession's broader contexts and its instrumental technocratic models.

Next, a case study of disruption in practice is developed, which examines the limitations of the instrumental technocratic.

Then there is an explanation of the role disruption played in my shift from instrumental technocratic to existential modes of practice.

The next part outlines an existential model and shows how it cohabits with the instrumental technocratic.

---

1 I am the CEO of an Australian consulting practice providing business succession advice and interventions to family owned businesses.
2 In this chapter, references to "my practice" or "the conventions of my practice" speak not only to my practice as CEO, but also to the practices of a larger group of consultants.

Finally, I demonstrate how the transformation of my conventions of practice emerged through my being-in-practice rather than thinking about practice from an objective distance.

Method

This chapter is written as an autoethnographic narrative. The reason is twofold:

- first, its central argument is developed around my reflection-in-practice of my lived experience of being-in-professional-practice; its narrative form is best accommodated as autoethnography.
- second, since this chapter is an exploration of my lived experience, interpretation, and search for professional meaning in the phenomenon of succession, this is done within a philosophical framework of existential hermeneutic phenomenology.

An autoethnographic narrative accommodates my lived experience as a succession practitioner. It enables me to speak about my particular conventions in practice. One's lived experience *in practice* is the legitimate concern of the autoethnographic researcher.

This chapter provides the space in which autoethnographic narrative and existentialism intersect. The intersection comes to life through what Holman Jones et al. (2013, p. 32) see as the compelling arguments for autoethnography, which include "working from insider knowledge". This means that autoethnographers use *personal* experience to create nuanced and detailed "thick descriptions" of *cultural* experience in order to facilitate understanding of these experiences (Geertz 1973). And so, too, my aims have been to provide rich and descriptive accounts of the succession experience and, in doing so, to show up the limitations of the instrumental technocratic. A further aim is to lead and facilitate changes to the conventions of practice of instrumentally technocratic succession practitioners.

My Lived Experience as a Succession Practitioner

The evolution of my conventions is situated in a philosophical practice whose methodology is grounded in Heidegger's hermeneutics. It can be characterized as a series of disclosures through disruption (1953, 2010).

As Segal (2015) points out, Heideggerian existential hermeneutic phenomenology provides a framework within which we might see disruptions in the conventions of our practice as the basis both to examine and rethink those conventions. Segal demonstrates how Heidegger maintains that whilst we are absorbed in the flow of our practice, we take the conventions of our practice for granted. It is in moments of being disrupted and estranged from our practice that we come to see the taken for granted conventions of our practice in such a way that we *can* rethink and critique them.

Although there was a series of disruptions that led me to rethink the taken for granted conventions underpinning *my* practice, I will focus more on one disruption or moment of estrangement. I will also show how disruptions and moments of estrangement in my clients' practices create the space for them to rethink the conventions underlying *their* practices. This chapter will operate on two parallel levels: disruption in the conventions of my practice and disruption in the practice of my clients. What I shall be offering is a way of working through disruption as the basis of succession planning for clients, and a way of working through disruption for practitioners who are engaged in succession planning. I shall begin with the latter and with my own experience of the disruption of conventions.

Based on the work of Heidegger, Segal (2015) also observes that working through an experience of disruption of conventions is a form of existential philosophical practice. I shall thus be conducting an activity of philosophical practice on my own conventions and providing the framework for an existential philosophical activity for succession clients and succession practitioners.

From a Heideggerian perspective I am my conventions. In specifically Heideggerian terms, Dasein's way of being is made up of its "average everyday" attunement to the world. What I am exploring is not the personality of the self (psychology) but the conventions or average everyday awareness (philosophy) of the being of my self.

The evolutionary transformation in my practice has seen my conventions of practice shift – from a predominantly instrumental and technocratic convention to an existential convention.

Instrumental solutions are essentially means-focused. Technocratic modes of practice are influenced and shaped by legislation, regulation, and the codes and conventions of practice of the particular disciplines in which these modes reside – that is, for example, in the practice of the law, and of accounting, and of financial planning. The technocratic is bounded by what Bryld (2000) sees as its focus on effectiveness and efficiency. This does not mean, however, that the technocratic is blind to the ends. In the life-world of succession, the means are operationalized under the umbrella of the technocratic.

On the other hand, existential solutions are focused on ends – that is, succession outcomes. However, a focus on ends does not mean that the existential

Figure 6.1 The Relationship between the Instrumental and the Technocratic

is blind to the means. There is a breadth to the existential view that balances the sharply focused instrumental technocratic.

Succession is less about means and ends than it is about what Gadamer (1989) describes as the fusion of horizons. Both means and ends in themselves are limited to their particular perspectives. Being in an existential process with another is about honouring the means. Having the ends in mind means that one is more open to horizons.

Gadamer (1989, pp. 301–2) wrote:

> The horizon is the range of vision that includes everything that can be seen from a particular vantage point. Applying this to the thinking mind, we speak of narrowness of horizon, of the possible expansion of horizon, of the opening up of new horizons, and so forth.

A person who has no horizon does not see far enough and hence over-values what is nearest to him. On the other hand, "to have horizon" means not being limited to what is nearby but being able to see beyond it. A person who knows his horizon knows the relative significance of everything within this horizon, whether it is near or far, great or small.

Widening my horizons, getting to the appropriate questions, and shifting my vantage point have brought about my shift. I have moved away from the horizons of the disciplinary – and regulatory-bound solutions put forward by other (instrumental technocratic) practitioners. The focus of those practitioners is fixed primarily on providing the means for succession: family charters; transactional contracts; wills; shareholder agreements; risk-based insurances; guidelines, processes, and checklists for successor selection and grooming, and so on. Each is based on some observable cause and effect. Each focuses on the means. All have limited horizons.

Existential succession practice accommodates the instrumental technocratic whilst working with its limitations. Commercial practicality is at work here. Without the instrumental technocratic, succession would fail for want of a mechanism to facilitate and support its commercial and functional transactions.

What is *it* that the instrumental technocratic does *not* deal with? To answer, I will describe an event that helped shift my thinking about my practice. However, to situate this event in its appropriate context, and to understand its role in shifting my thinking, I will describe the prior development of my practice.

I had shaped a means-focused approach to succession. It was instrumental, holistic and well received by clients. It had been praised by academics who reviewed it (Barrett and Dunemann 2004a). Yet, there were unseen limitations that meant a lengthy sales cycle and uneven engagement by clients once the journey commenced.

I realized, after reflecting on one particular client meeting, that my assumptions about their succession were wrong. I was thrown. I had assumed: first, that they *wanted* to exit from their business and they had a plan in place for their life after it; and, second, that they were financially motivated to extract the maximum value of their business so they could fund their retirement (CPA 2004). My discovery disrupted my conventions of practice. I had been blinded by my assumptions. I was missing key information. Not financial data – rather, something that might speak to *who* succession clients *were*, and *who they wanted to be* post-succession.

I was also thrown by a sense of professional frustration. This came from seeing two things in succession clients: firstly, a lack of engagement with the concept of succession; secondly, an on-again, off-again commitment to my process. Was it not a model and a process that we had discussed? Did this not clearly show them what was required for a financially secure succession? What could they not see? Why were they not "bolted on" to my succession process?

I had a felt sense that some simple questions might uncover the missing data and provide a partial solution to my professional frustration. The questions I posed were: first, "For all of your time in business what would be the business legacy you would like to leave behind?"; second, "Who do you want to become when you've exited your business?"; and, third, "What does your succession and exit from your business *really mean* to you?"

I "road tested" these questions and found that succession clients were *looking for meaning* in their succession. A framework for opening up to meaning took shape:

Question	Response to meaning
"For all of your time in business what would be the business legacy you would like to leave behind?"	I want to leave behind a A profitable and sustainable business An enduring brand A team and a culture that I've created An unsullied personal and business reputation
"Who do you want to be when you've exited your business?"	I want to be someone with a continuing role to play – not necessarily as a volunteer, but as a mentor
"What does your succession and exit from your business *really mean* to you?"	A time of change and transition This concerns me – it's daunting even terrifying

As this was used in practice, two themes emerged:

- First,
  - clients disclosed apprehension and uncertainty about their physical mortality and their business mortality; and
  - they were existentially anxious about their loss of a sense of purpose and their identity.

- Second, their desire to leave behind a legacy (inter alia) of an *unsullied personal and business reputation* disclosed a range of vulnerabilities – including, though not limited to, the sadness of estrangement from their children. For many clients, resolving these vulnerabilities becomes an *end* in itself.

This framework opened up the possibilities for new conventions of practice. It stood in apposition to my familiar conventions and to what I understood were best-practice instrumental technocratic succession conventions. This is because what was crystallizing for me was an important understanding of what were the "real" ends clients were seeking in and through their succession. Within that, there had emerged for me a nascent understanding of the importance to succession clients of their gaining a sense of *meaning* in their succession. The existential questions described earlier, and the answers given by succession clients, opened up the possibilities for discovering their sense of meaning. The context for this is situated in succession clients leaving one purposeful life-context for another.

An existential framework in which succession clients can create meaning for themselves is reflective of the nature of meaning as discussed by existential philosophers. Kierkegaard spoke about meaning as coming from purpose: "What I really need is to get clear about what I must do, not what I must know . . . What matters is to find a purpose (which) must come alive in me" (1978, p. 34). For Sartre, meaning comes from purpose: "Man is nothing else than that which he makes of himself" (1948, 1973, p. 28). But, more challengingly, purpose emerges through choice – an existential dilemma: "life has no meaning *a priori* . . . it is up to you to give it a meaning, and value is nothing but the meaning that you choose" (1947, p. 58).

Failure to choose is an act of self-deception – or "bad faith" as Sartre calls it. Self-deception is one of the key elements sitting at the core of the succession dilemma: it is one of the things that leaves succession clients standing at the edge of the succession abyss – unable or unwilling to jump it. The "fact" of their arriving at the point where they need to do something about their succession is both observable, but unbelievable, to them. This sense of unbelievability hinders their doing anything about their succession. In Sartrean terms this is an act of self-deception or "bad faith" because succession clients' ageing (and the gradual decline in their cognition required to run a business) and their death cannot be escaped. As Sartre explains, "the first act of bad faith is to flee what it can not flee, to flee what it is" (2003, p. 93). The existential framework I have developed opens up the issues of meaning, purpose, and choice – and offers clients ways to move beyond bad faith and self-deception. Finally, Frankl observed that "the meaning of life differs from man to man, from day to day, and from hour to hour. What matters, therefore, is not the meaning of life in general but rather the specific meaning of a person's life at a given moment" (1946, 1959, p. 113). This serves as an important reminder that in practice an existential framework for succession works with the nuances and idiosyncrasies of each individual client and not to some pre-set instrumental, technocratic formula.

Discovering the questions and themes did not mean that the framework was settled and static. It continues to evolve dynamically through moments of disruption and estrangement in practice. Described elsewhere in this chapter, it is consistent with Segal's observation that it is through such moments of estrangement that "we come to see the taken for granted conventions of our practice such that we can rethink and critique them" (Segal 2015).

The framework provided some interest to me, and through reflection I began a rethink and critique of my conventions. An important in-practice question is not "why don't the existing practitioner and academic models of succession practice work as well as they might?" Rather, the questions are: "If the existing instrumental models are missing the mark, how can they be enhanced to bring them closer to it? What are they missing?"

The answer is that the extant models were speaking neither to the concerns of succession clients nor to their search for meaning. These are existential in their nature. And they allow me access to the disclosive spaces that Heidegger (1953, 2010) says are essential to understanding being-in the world.

My framework reaches into the existential. I did not immediately see that. My exposure to existentialism was limited to undergraduate studies of Sartre – and long recessed in my mind. Existentially, the questions emerged from my felt sense that something was missing. I was curious to find the missing piece.

It was only after I commenced my doctoral research that I became reacquainted with the existential and its fit with my thinking. "Fit" evolved through my attunement to the emotions (or mood) of succession clients, as well as a greater appreciation of succession's existential dimensions.

It soon became apparent to me that these questions were pointers to underlying anxieties. They opened up the space for me to work with the existential anxieties of succession clients. These anxieties fit with Yalom's (1980) description of existential anxieties as the four ultimate concerns of life: death, freedom, isolation, and meaninglessness. Popovic (2002, p. 32) suggests that *existential* anxiety refers to uncertainties relating to the human condition, existence itself. In speaking about the existential literature and its considerable attention to the fundamental role of anxiety (Heidegger, 1953, 2010; Kierkegaard, 1944; May 1950; Sartre 2003). van Deurzen-Smith says that in "this tradition anxiety is seen as an inevitable part of human living . . . It is the sensation that accompanies self-consciousness and awareness of one's vulnerability when confronted with the possibility of one's death. It is therefore the *sine qua non* of facing life and finding oneself" (1988, p. 38).

Existential anxieties disrupt clients' succession and my conventions of practice. This is illustrated by another event that threw me.

I attended the funeral of a fifty-seven year old friend, Paul. He was the second-generation owner of the family business that had been a part of his whole life. It had shaped his identity, given him his sense of purpose, and provided *meaning* to him.

Exactly one week after the sale of the business, his wife found him hanging, dead, in the garage.

His death shocked me. I was given a copy of his suicide note. His note disrupted my assumptions about succession and my enacted succession practice. In honouring the privilege of receiving his note, I have worked since then to change my assumptions and my conventions of practice.

Simply, the key question for me had become: how could my existing instrumental technocratic conventions shift in order to embrace succession clients' search for *meaning* in, and beyond, their succession?

Paul's note revealed existential anxieties: loss of identity; erosion of his sense of life-purpose; and uncertainty about who he was to become. Clearly there had been a failure to deal with these significant issues. I saw a weakness in my conventions of practice and in those of other practitioners.

I was surprised by how far I was thrown. It took me closer to understanding the potentialities of existential anxieties and their role in shaping succession.

Two dimensions have since framed my rethinking my practice. First, and existentially, I had a felt sense that the existing models were not robust enough to deal with existential disruptions. Second, that felt sense opened an understanding that existential disruption comes from the humanness of succession. By humanness I mean that succession involves human beings whose vulnerabilities are exposed and whose anxieties are disclosed to themselves and to others.

As a succession practitioner I came to realize that the complexities of succession are not solvable through instrumental technocratic conventions of practice. This chapter describes how my realization has underpinned the evolution of my conventions and habits of succession practice. They have shifted beyond the instrumental technocratic towards the existential.

I have not set out to replace the instrumental technocratic. This would be disingenuous as that model underpins the legal, transactional, and financial dimensions of succession. Rather, my purpose has been to deliver new conventions and habits of practice that enhance, and cohabit with, the instrumental technocratic. Cohabitation of models and conventions fits with what Gadamer (1989) meant when he described a fusion of horizons.

The Context of Succession and its Instrumental Technocratic Models

Succession in Context

Business succession is the transfer of the management and/or control of a business (Ip and Jacobs 2006). It sees "the passing of the leadership baton from the founder-owner to a successor who will either be a family member or a non-family member; that is, a 'professional manager'" (Beckhard and Burke 1983, p. 3).

Global estimates of the number of family owned and privately owned businesses suggest they comprise between 80 per cent and 98 per cent of all enterprises (Poza 2010). The MGI Family and Private Business Survey (Smyrnios and Dana 2006) noted that the family business sector in Australia accounted for $4.3 trillion in aggregate wealth, and that 81 per cent of their owners intend to retire in the next ten years generating a wealth transfer of $3.5 trillion.

The relationship between wealth-creation and economic and industrial capacity, and the changing demographics through the ageing of business owners, underpin the importance of business succession.

The economic significance of the family business sector is at risk if these demographic and generational issues cannot be resolved. How family business succession is planned, executed, and managed across the sector is critical to its longevity, resilience, and prosperity. There are compelling reasons to examine the efficacy of extant succession models and to open up the possibility of alternative and/or complementary models.

These complementary, different, and alternative models need not replace the predominant instrumental model. But, they can enhance it through co-existence and collaboration in both the academic and practitioner settings.

The Extant Models in the Literature and in Practice: An Instrumental Technocratic Approach to Succession

What are the current conventions of family business succession? What are succession's key influences in the literature and in practice?

Business succession is well represented in the literatures of entrepreneurship and business strategy. Its principle home is situated in the literature of family business that is now regarded as a legitimate field of enquiry (Barrett and Dunemann 2004b; Handler 1994; Ip and Jacobs 2006) and *a discipline in its own right* (emphasis mine). This has been echoed more recently by Carney and Jaskiewicz who have tracked "the development of family business as a fringe subject initially located at the margins of scholarly attention towards its emergence as a mainstream subject in the organization sciences that is now fully engaged with important contemporary questions relevant to both managers and policy communities" (2014, p. 3).

Much of the dominant succession literature is centred on "process": its rationale, domains of influence (for example, economics, firm performance, psychology, etc), its implications, and its consequences. This is also a feature of the succession models considered by Baù et al. who note that "Sharma and colleagues (2003) recognize that too often succession planning is driven by means rather than ends. Generally, the reason for succession planning is the necessity of formalizing the presence of a trusted successor rather than the need for succession to preserve the family firm" (Baù et al. 2013).

The literature has spawned a range of linear, instrumental technocratic succession models.

What is Instrumentalism?

The definition of instrumental reasoning used here is taken partially from Shirley Pendlebury's (1990) article, "Practical Arguments and Situational Appreciation in Teaching". Pendlebury claims that technical reasoning occurs "where ends are well defined and deliberation is solely or primarily concerned with finding the most efficient means to bring about the end" (1990, p. 174).

In adding to Pendlebury's claim, my argument in this chapter is that not only is reasoning technical or instrumental where the ends are well defined but where there is an *omission of discussing the ends in relation to the means*. I follow Pendlebury's argument that, in instrumental reasoning, the means become the central focus of concern. A failure to work with the ends in relation to the means is a limitation of the instrumental. This speaks to Gadamer's (1989) notion of "narrowed horizon". It sees the instrumental technocratic "over value what is nearest" (Gadamer 1989) and, perhaps, ignores or limits the possibilities and potentialities that open up for succession clients when the ends are seen in relation to the means.

In contrast to the instrumental form of reasoning, an existential, or what Pendlebury calls a constitutive, form of reasoning is needed. Constitutive or existential reasoning focuses not only on the means but also on the means *in relation to* the ends. Indeed, it puts them in a circular relationship to each other in which means and ends are in a mutually clarifying relationship. It speaks to the clarification of meaning which comes from the circularity imagined by Gendlin's practice of reflective listening (1996, p. 45) which is discussed further in below. In constitutive and existential reasoning the means are clarified in relation to the ends and the ends are made more explicit in relation to the means. Writing about constitutive reasoning in the context of teaching Pendlebury says: "In examining the strength of a teacher's practical arguments we look not only at whether the means were appropriately chosen, but also at whether the ends were appropriately specified. It is possible for a teacher to choose her means well and yet not be a competent practitioner" (1990, p. 178).

Pendlebury's claim applies in all means-end relationships not only in the context of teaching. The claim that I make in the context of succession is that it is possible to be precise and clear about the means without choosing the ends well. This is the danger of an instrumental form of rationality: it focuses primarily on the means and not on the cyclical relationship between means and ends. In contrast to this, existential forms of reasoning are always focused on the ends, or the purposes, and the relationship between the ends and means and means and ends. This cyclical relationship is a hermeneutic form of relationship and is present in existential conventions of succession practice.

This relationship works with Gadamer's horizons. The dynamic nature of this relationship sees its to-ing and fro-ing between means and ends, allowing clients and practitioners to look backwards and live forwards (Kierkegaard, 2000), and expand their horizons or open up new horizons (Gadamer 1989).

In the next part, I will demonstrate that instrumental forms of reasoning have dominated the succession literature. The prevailing focus in this literature is on legal, accounting, and organizational arrangements, and on concepts including agency theory, stakeholder theory, and the resource-based view of the firm. This also has been recognized by Baù et al. (2013, p. 176), and this focus in the literature has an emphasis on process rather than on the discussion of the cyclical relationship between the means and the ends desired by the owner/s in their transition from business. It is often the case that the owner in transition does not have a clear sense of the ends beyond a vague idea of exit and retirement. Indeed, the aim of this chapter in general is to show that means and ends can be used to clarify each other.

Instrumental models are technocratic. They are framed by legislation, regulations, and codes of conduct. As an example, in New South Wales, their advice is formulated to meet the legislative and regulatory requirements of the *Succession Act (NSW), 2006*, the *Corporations Act (Commonwealth) 2001*, the *Income Tax Assessment Act (Commonwealth) 1997* and *The Financial Services Reform Act (Commonwealth) 2001*. Practitioners are signatories to their professional codes of conduct such as those mandated for professional registration by bodies such as the NSW Law Society (lawyers), the Institute of Chartered Accountants (accountants), and the Financial Planning Association (financial planners).

Instrumentalism is tied to rationality and rule-formulation. Advice given, or judgments made, in an instrumental, rational context are dependent on an observable cause–effect relationship. These are seen often in the models of succession practice that are relied on by succession advisers like lawyers, accountants, financial planners, risk advisers, and business brokers.

Instrumentalism is built on positivist, scientific principles. Instrumentalism represents a means-to-ends approach, concerned with the means and not the ends nor the relationship between means and ends. Instrumentalism informs the disciplines from which succession practitioners derive much of their knowledge, their conventions of practice, and their applied models. The law and accounting are examples. Financial planning is another. These are professional disciplines bounded by instrumental rationality. Instrumentalism creates their epistemology and shapes their practice. As a result, instrumentalism has shaped the habits and conventions of succession practice.

In their review of the succession literature, Barrett and Dunemann (2004b) identified seven models. I suggest these models further exemplify the instrumental technocratic approach in both their design and their application. They are:

1   succession as a relay (Dyck et al. 2002);
2   relationships (Fox et al. 1996);
3   feedback and assessment (Burke 2003);
4   the five rules model (Hamilton 2003);
5   the four phases model (Kirschner and Kirschner 2000);
6   identification, selection, mentoring, and planning (Sharma et al. 2000); and
7   the integrative model (Le Breton-Miller et al. 2004).

These models all emphasize means to achieve ends. They rely on cause–effect without regards to the dynamic and circular relationship between means and ends, and fits the view of Baù et al. (2013) which has been noted earlier.

Instrumental models as described in the literature have been brought into and adapted to in-practice use by succession practitioners. Tax and estate planning afford much of the disciplinary focus (Ip and Jacobs 2006) and these disciplines too are grounded in scientific principles and instrumental rationality.

In practice, instrumentalism seems to practitioners the obvious source of succession solutions. As an instrumentally rational practitioner, Day (nd, pp. 9–10) observes that the succession adviser's task is the collection and use of quantitative data: assets and liabilities; schedules of personal and business debt; personal and business insurances, and so on. Day's locus of attention is the management of both risk and the financial dimensions of succession.

Another example of instrumental rationality in practice occurs with the suggestion that succession starts with eleven key steps, eight of which are clearly instrumental technocratic (I/T):

1   personal goals and vision for the transfer of ownership and management;
2   identification of a successor and their skills (I/T);
3   consideration of family involvement in leadership and ownership of the company;
4   tax (I/T);
5   liquidity (I/T);
6   a shareholder buy–sell agreement (I/T);
7   contingency plans in the event of an owner's becoming disabled (I/T);
8   corporate structures(I/T);
9   retirement cash-flow needs (I/T);
10   business valuation(I/T);
11   post-transfer involvement and a creative retirement structure (Holland 2008).

Figures 6.2, 6.3, and 6.4 model instrumental approaches and their adaptation to a range of practitioner interests.

Figure 6.2 shows an instrumentally rational approach structured around managing and achieving key financial outcomes:

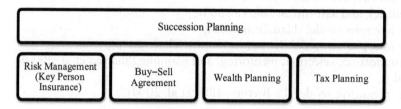

Figure 6.2 Instrumental Succession as a Financial-based Process

Figure 6.3 extends the model's focus beyond the financial outcomes to consideration of the exiting owner planning for their active retirement:

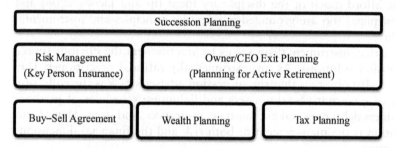

Figure 6.3 Instrumental Succession Combining Financial Outcomes with Owner Preparation

In Figure 6.4, we are introduced to two additional concepts: (i) transaction planning and value building, and (ii) successor grooming. Many practitioners see each of these as an important element of the overall succession solution. Figure 6.4 is a visual representation of the holistic model of succession practice which had been reviewed for my firm by Barrett and Dunemann (2004a):

Each model in Figures 6.2 to 6.4 assumes a linear, instrumental technocratic approach. At a rational level, they all make sense. They promise highly functional and observable succession outcomes. But none deals with the contingencies and uncertainties which mark the existential, lived experience of succession.

An instrumental approach does little to solve an important succession puzzle that is captured by my question: "Why does it seem the majority of owners does not engage in or recognize the need to do something about their succession?" In noting the importance of this issue, Glassop et al. (2006; 2007; 2008; 2005) also

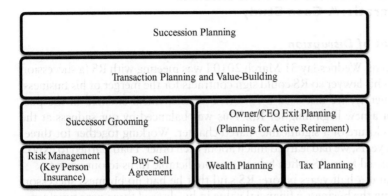

Figure 6.4 An Instrumental Succession Model Combining Financial, Owner, Successor, and Transaction

observe that a spike in owners' succession awareness is followed by a decline. My observation from practice is that this phenomenon speaks to the notion that, in a Heideggerian sense, the owners' everyday coping with the uncertainty of their succession is to dilute, prevaricate, or postpone their engagement with it. And, there is a risk that disengaged owners will have a flawed succession – or none at all. (They will hesitate on the edge of Sartre's abyss!)

Earlier I noted that for Ip and Jacobs (2006) succession is the haunt of lawyers and accountants. For them, succession is about an instrumental transition that satisfies financial and legal criteria. This is a constrained and narrow-horizoned approach that risks succession stakeholders being blind-sided.

It is not an approach that deals well with the existential disruption that emerges through the humanness of the succession experience.

Existential disruption and humanness presented a challenge to my familiar ways of operating. My response was to develop a different approach to succession. In doing so, I turned to Martin Heidegger, the German philosopher whose seminal work on existential hermeneutics is *Being and Time* (1953, 2010). In simple terms, Heidegger's existential hermeneutics comprises two themes. In the first, we are concerned with the existential nature of human life – its meaning or its lack of meaning. Paul's suicide presents a stark example of where and how a business owner in succession finds (or fails to find) meaning. In the second (hermeneutics), we are concerned with looking for *truth* in a context in which our interpretation is influenced by our preconceptions, our self-understanding, and our understanding of the world. For Paul, this was defined by the life-world of the family business that had subsumed him. His preconceptions, self-understanding, and understanding of the world were all influenced by his attachment to and relationship with the family business. He found it difficult to see beyond his life in it. His horizons (Gadamer 1989) were narrowed.

The Limitations of the Instrumental Technocratic: A Case Study

A Moment of Disruption

At 3.45pm on Wednesday 31 March 2010 I was meeting with RS (a succession client) and his lawyer so RS could sign contracts for the merger of his business.

Subsequently, we disclosed a felt sense of excitement situated in the possibilities of a new beginning for RS. This was balanced by our sadness at the imminent closure of a significant, shared chapter. Working together for three-and-a-half years, we had learned much about each other. I had learned to expect the unexpected from RS, often bringing unpredictable turns to our course.

Three-and-a-half years before, RS said that he had no business successor. Maximizing the business's financial value in his desired three-year timeframe for exit made unlikely an internal sale. And he was looking for an exit.

RS's business was a highly successful, niche-based engineering consultancy. The engineering sector had shrunk through aggregation by larger firms looking to replace through acquisition the revenues lost during the Global Financial Crisis (GFC).

RS felt constrained by the thought that the size of his business would be unattractive to a buyer. Externally, his firm was known for: strong, profitable revenues; high work volumes; well-regarded professional staff; high brand awareness and brand equity; and a large, client base of repeat customers. His was a highly saleable business in a market hungry for acquisitions.

RS had disclosed to me his personal world: one of isolation and emptiness with "every waking hour" spent in his business over 25 years. He had a home office and an external office. He felt trapped. His home office had become his preferred place. He could not separate home from work.

RS had disclosed regret that his business commitment over-shadowed and fractured his relationships: two ex-wives; estranged adult children; a diminished social circle; and no-one that he would call a friend.

This disclosure occurred during a poignant conversation in his home office. I noticed a set of very expensive golf clubs and asked if he would play more golf once he had exited his business. He replied: "To enjoy golf, you need to play with friends. I don't have any friends." I asked him what he meant: no golf-playing friends – or no friends. "No friends at all – some acquaintances – but most 'friends' are really in my wife's social circle. I have no-one to whom I can confide, share a laugh, or dream with."

Two important pointers for our relationship and for his succession strategy emerged. First, both relationship and strategy were influenced by existential anxiety caused by his friendlessness. Second, his disclosure disrupted my familiar way of dealing with succession. My response is outlined later.

His succession required a parallel strategy: the one (instrumental technocratic) focused on his business. The other (existential) focused on his preparations for life after business – including finding friendships.

The former was relatively simple: (i) tidy up the balance sheet; (ii) codify the business processes and intellectual property; and (iii) shape a transaction that would meet the needs of both parties. This requirement was met through generous financial terms.

The existential strategy was far from straightforward.

RS had reached an age and stage where he wanted to transition out of both management and ownership. His interest in mentoring young people led to a role post-merger: mentoring the firm's new graduates.

He had an engineer's pedantic eye for detail that he brought into each review of the documents. He received the final document on the morning of 31 March 2010 – settlement day. His legal advisers and I were satisfied. He had not given any indication of discomfort.

At 3.45pm the lawyer asked RS to sign the documents – a formality! With pen poised and turning the pages, RS marked up items saying "No. No. Didn't agree to that. No. Definitely not . . . "

Throwing his pen on the table he said, "You know what? I'm out. I'm not going to go ahead." Another surprise turn!

Had we followed an instrumental path, the transaction would have ended there.

Resolving Disruption by Shifting from the Instrumental Technocratic to the Existential

Like the others, this disruption emerged from RS's disclosures of isolation, emptiness, entrapment, regret, and friendlessness. None of these was resolvable through instrumental technocratic approaches.

I felt and heard his anxiety. I reassured him that whilst withdrawal might be "ugly", it was okay if he thought it best. I offered him five minutes to reflect alone on his decision and its consequences.

One of my re-thought conventions in practice was to have clients keep a journal. In his, RS had begun to imagine his life post-business. We called it "his book". As I left him to reflect, I said: "It's fine to walk away from this. And it's best to do so now. But, I'm just wondering, how will you ever bring your personal vision to life, and how will you complete your book?"

He looked at me, stood, and with tears welling, said, "OK. I'm in. I don't want to lose my future that I've written in my book." He picked up his pen, initialled every page, and signed off with a flourish. The deal was done!

What changed his mind? What was the tipping point that shifted him from being "out" to being "in"?

To answer, I will illustrate just how far my conventions of practice had moved towards the existential.

RS's journal was a blue, linen-bound notebook I had given him. It became a safe space for him to reflect on three existential themes: (i) the business legacy he would most like to leave; (ii) the creation of a new identity and a fresh sense of purpose and meaning; and (iii) dealing with feelings of loss and grief as he left his business.

Around the first theme, RS imagined a four-part business legacy: (i) a profitable and sustainable business; (ii) an enduring brand; (iii) a team and a culture that he had created and sustained; and (iv) an unsullied personal and business reputation.

Journaling provided the emotional scaffold for the work that needed to be done in and on the business to create value and to smooth the way for his exit. This scaffold was a prompt for keeping our discussions with potential acquirers on track.

RS met the second and third existential themes in his journal as he fleshed out (as I had asked) his imaginings of his next life-stage. Journaling allowed him to develop a well-articulated, clear narrative. It provided a place where he could reflect on his succession. And it informed him when he needed to take some tough decisions. He described a future vision of himself that was full of possibilities awaiting discovery. His narrative became the compass that helped him stay on course.

The journal housed a future life that admitted friends and confidants. Through sharing his journal and narrative with me, I was privileged to peer through a window at his existential anxieties. This opened up ways for me to deal iteratively with both RS's existential anxieties and the disruptions *I* had experienced as a result. The insights I gained prompted me to reflect, critique, and rethink my habits and conventions of practice.

One of RS's existential anxieties centred on the absence of close, trusted friends. He had no-one in whom he could confide. I had heard this type of story before. And I was confident that through my familiar conventions we would find the friends he was seeking.

Confidants are neither stakeholders in succession nor subjectively wedded to its outcomes. Confidants play an important role bringing to clients' succession experience a sense of balanced objectivity and "real-world" ways of everyday coping. These are enormously valuable to clients confronted by significant, imminent, and disruptive changes to their business and work lives. Because of this, they are sought and welcomed by clients into their life-world.

I did not anticipate the next disruption which played out as RS's strong resistance to the possibility of discovering his own confidants: "There's no-one"; "I don't think I could trust anyone"; "I don't like getting too close to people"; "I don't have the time"; "No – this just won't work for me"; "You are just wasting your time if you think I'll do something that I don't want."

In the moment, I was not sure how to respond. I felt a sense of powerlessness. How useful was my familiar when he was disclosing a deep and painful emptiness? His constant anchor was his business. He was disrupted by the prospect of separating from the very thing that had defined him, shaped his self-worth, and told his life-world who he was. And this disruption was heightened by his friendlessness.

As I reflected on his discomfort, I resolved to work with him to imagine more clearly the possibilities of finding future friendships and, with that, the imaginings of a life well spent. This required cautious patience.

Journaling opened the space for RS to visualize in words or in pictures an extended social circle whose core was a group of confidants. He could "see" them. He could "see" how he might find new, trusted friends. And, over time, he did. He began to test with those trusted others the business and life changes he was facing. He lifted his narrative from its pages and shared it with them. He was finding new sources of meaning and sense-making.

We regularly reviewed his narrative. This created further opportunities for discourse and imaginings. Sometimes we were both surprised by what was revealed. Discourse helped reduce ambiguity, uncertainty, and anxiety about the direction in which we were heading, and created for both of us a sense-making context.

Narrative-centred discourse enabled me to work more closely with the raw materials that were emerging. For example, RS disclosed a great depth of concern about his reputation: "What will my staff think about me selling? I don't want them to think that I am abandoning them." "What will the purchasers think of me? Will they try to change things because we haven't done them well enough?" Whilst these questions do not, on the surface, indicate a crisis in RS, they do represent anxiety that could disrupt the transaction's momentum. My familiar response to his first question would have been to suggest that an announcement would suffice. Employees seem to have well-trained antennae which inform them that "something's up" when they see "suits" wandering through their workplace. They put two-and-two together to know what's happening.

RS's concern about his reputation internally and his wish to appear not to abandon his employees, prompted a decision that RS would host a staff dinner. There he would reveal his thinking about his planned exit, suggest a three-year timeframe, and announce the formation of a transition group to keep staff up-to-date. These were a part of my familiar. My shift in conventions also prompted him to open a conversation he had never had with employees: by simply asking for their *understanding and help*. This conversation delivered very positive outcomes. No employees were lost in the period pre- or post-merger. Productivity increased. Profitability was enhanced. And RS's reputation was unblemished.

His self-doubt, his constrained thinking about the value of his business, and his fear that a purchaser would discount their price was dealt with more pragmatically. The assets the acquirers most wanted were: intellectual property, clients, and human resources. We developed and role-played a "script" to provide him with the confidence to qualitatively describe and quantitatively substantiate the value of those key assets. It described the value in RS's work processes and practices. The script helped ease his self-doubt.

One early transformative lesson for me was the significance to RS of telling me his story (myth making about himself) and in being curious about his possibilities. These are existential activities which are discussed by May (1991; 1994) and Heidegger (1953, 2010; 1985).

The importance of crafting and telling stories (myths) draws on May's finding that, "A myth is a way of making sense in a senseless world. Myths are narrative patterns that give significance to our existence . . . Myth making is essential in gaining mental health" (1991, p. 17). May observed that "the chief problem of people in the middle decade of the twentieth century is *emptiness*" (2009, p. 4). May also suggested "we experience ourselves as a thinking-intuiting-feeling and acting unity. The self is thus not merely the sum of the various 'roles' one plays – it is the capacity by which one *knows* he plays those roles; it is the center from which one sees and is aware of these so-called different 'sides' of himself" (2009, p. 64).

May's observations are important to understanding how RS could make sense when his world was being turned upside down. How could he avoid an existential emptiness? And how might he adopt new, different roles and identities when those he's known, and been known for, are removed?

The answers were found through my using new conventions in my succession practice. These allowed me to stay in relationship with RS. As a whole, they are circular in nature: discourse, listening, discovery, reflection, disclosure, and writing:

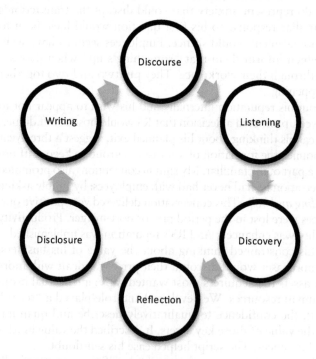

Figure 6.5 Relational Conventions of Practice

Conversation provided opportunities for disclosure and discovery. Listening as a part of conversation is an important tool. Heidegger (1953, 2010) writes that listening is constitutive for discourse and is an important part of understanding and being-in the world. These were key parts of our working together.

As I worked with RS's myths and narrative, I found that I learned lessons for my practice. These enabled me to respond to disruptions to my conventions of practice that appeared at each moment of RS's existential anxiety. These surprised me, and often threw me. Rather than being stuck in my surprise or thrown-ness, my habit of practice became one of moving with the dynamic flow within and outside the hermeneutic circle of RS's succession.

One such disruption occurred through RS's lack of confidence in the completion of the sale "because no-one would want to buy a business of this size" or "because of something I haven't done". When he was tiring of the due diligence process or the merger negotiations, his self-doubt re-emerged: "They'll find something wrong"; "They'll knock the price down to something I cannot reasonably accept"; "I'm not sure they are serious – maybe we should just give up and I'll simply close the doors and walk away."

Journaling his myth and narrative provided existential clues I could use to keep him on track. He had written that he envisioned opportunities to: look back with a sense of achievement and say, "I created that"; mentor young graduates; be freed to travel; be financially rewarded; and be free of risk.

By opening up his myth and narrative RS invited me to dive into his experience. And by immersing myself *in* it I was better able to understand and respond to his anxieties. This response emerges from what Gadamer (1980) describes as Socrates' "guiding a person through thoughtful discussion" (1980, p. 3) in which there is a "reciprocal relationship between the line of his argument on the one hand and the level of insight of his partners in the discussion on the other" (1980, p. 1). This Socratic, reciprocal relationship also speaks to Gendlin's (1996) notion of reflective listening that is outlined briefly below. The space for such a relationship is situated in an existential mode of succession practice.

The Existential Model and its Embrace of the Instrumental Technocratic

There is a joke about consultants: they are the people who take your watch to tell you the time. As my practice transformed, I discovered the importance of leaving my clients' watches in place, getting them to work out the time for themselves, and then telling me the time.

The blue linen notebook became the place where RS found ways to work out the time for himself. It was here that he was able to discover *his* possibilities and, within *his* possibilities, many answers about his future life.

For Heidegger, possibilities provide a way of everyday coping. "Why does the understanding . . . always press forward into possibilities? It is because the understanding has in itself the existential structure which we call '*projection*'" (1953, 2010). Dreyfus (1991) observed that "Coping with the available proceeds by pressing into possibilities". Possibilities are more than choices. In Heidegger, possibilities are representative of different ways-of-being – our "can-be or ability-to-be" (Dreyfus and Wrathall 2005, 2007, p. 6).

There is circularity at work here. The possibilities confronting succession clients are informed by their pre-dispositions which emerge from their past experience. These are shaped by who/what they want to become. Heidegger writes: "Every potentiality-to-be for something is a determined confrontation [*Auseinandersetzung*] with what has been [*Gewesenes*], in view of something coming toward me [*Zukommendes*], and to which I am resolved" (1997, 2001, pp. 158–9).

Heidegger's notion of possibilities opens new conventions for my practice. Since the journals contain clients' potentialities, they become the means through which clients can cope with the contingencies and unexpectedness of their succession ends. Their potentiality-to-be emerges from two of the three key questions I ask of them: first, their legacy question: "for all of your time in business, what is the legacy you would most like to leave behind?"; and, second, their "identity" question: "who do you want to become in your transition from this business?" Working with possibilities has become a habit of my practice.

I invite clients to give freedom to their curiosity through their journaling as their narratives and myths emerge. Curiosity enables clients to imagine new roles, new purpose, new beginnings, and new meanings in their life after succession. Heidegger (1953, 2010) says of curiosity that it "is everywhere and nowhere. This mode of being-in-the-world reveals a new kind of being of everyday Dasein" (i.e. the concept that humans exist in the world *and* inhabit it). Heidegger suggests that curiosity is a tendency "(which) is the care for the discovery and the bringing-near of what is not yet experienced or of what is not an everyday experience, the care of being 'away from' the constantly and immediately available things . . . This means that it does not dwell on something definitely and thematically grasped, but prefers characteristically to jump from one thing to another, a feature which is constitutive of curiosity" (1985). Existential curiosity becomes important to succession clients as I encourage them to discover new "modes of being", of finding and doing things that may be different to and distant from their now familiar life-worlds.

Curiosities and possibilities open up the space for conversation. The practice of listening to clients' stories and learning about their possibilities is an existential experience. As noted earlier, Heidegger (1953, 2010) says "listening is constitutive for discourse" and the "connection of discourse with understanding and intelligibility becomes clear through an existential possibility which belongs to discourse itself, listening". Listening has always been important in my practice.

However, the transformative steps towards an existential practice have included adopting a habit of practice based on what Gendlin (1996) has described as reflective listening. This is *not* the same as that which is meant when we speak of "reflective practice". Nor does it does mean my reflection *on* what has been said. Rather, Gendlin means that the listener's response to what has been said is to mirror it (that is, make a reflection *of what's been said*) in further conversation. This is done by "saying back exactly what the person is trying to convey" (Gendlin 1996, p. 45). Gendlin reminds us that we "cannot usually grasp exactly what another person means the first time something is said" (1996, p. 45). This speaks again to the Socratic approach of establishing meaning through reciprocity. It is an interpretive listening that requires one to be non-judgmental. Gendlin (1996, p. 11) suggests that reflective listening helps avoid dead-end discussions. A benefit of reflective listening as a habit of practice is that clients stay on their own natural track. And, as a result, practitioners also stay on the desired track heading towards the clients' ends.

My felt sense was that my clients' myths and their imaginings of their future life would effectively bookend the way in which they might cope with the roller coaster ride of succession. I have found through my practice that the writing of their narrative (i.e. their myth), and their being curious to future possibilities, have provided sufficient pieces for them to solve their succession puzzle. Existentially, this helps clients remove their self-imposed barriers to succession. It works to dilute dissonance and anxieties.

Just as I "found" Heidegger and existentialism, I also (re)discovered journaling. My earliest use of journaling was during my period of high-school teaching. There I used journaling as a way of working with students to unlock their imagination, their creative curiosity, and their potential for writing.

As a practitioner involved in a process of transformation-of-practice, I was looking for a rationale to bring journaling into succession practice since I had evidenced the benefits of journaling during my teaching. I was looking for a connection between journaling and my curiosity of its value as a habit of practice. My search took me to the field of narrative therapy in which journaling was widely used. I was struck by the sense that there was a similarity between my relationship with my clients and the therapist–client relationship.

This means that my appropriation to my succession practice of a practice from another discipline (Spinosa et al. 1997, p. 4) saw me borrowing from narrative therapy and from the work of Epston and White (1990), Freedman and Combs (1996), and White (1997). Narrative therapy "seeks to be a respectful, non-blaming approach to counseling and community work, which centres people as the experts in their own lives. It views problems as separate from people and assumes people have many skills, competencies, beliefs, values, commitments and abilities that will assist them to reduce the influence of problems in their lives" (Morgan 2000).

In her work on journal writing and qualitative research, Janesick (1998) describes the work of Ira Progoff. Janesick notes that, as a therapist, "Most recently, Ira Progoff (1975) has written of an intensive journal. Progoff developed a set of techniques which provide a structure for keeping a journal and a springboard for development (which) is a journal for unlocking one's creativity and coming to terms with one's self. The intensive journal method is a reflective, in-depth process of writing, speaking what is written, and in some cases sharing what is written with others" (Janesick 1998, p. 8).

Of course, the use of journaling need not be undertaken only in the context of therapy. But the method has become a habit amongst my new conventions of succession practice because it provides a framework for succession clients to unlock their creativity and come to terms with themselves – an important step in their everyday coping with the existential anxieties of succession.

As a fellow traveller on RS's journey, I engaged him in conversation, asked him questions only he could answer, and reviewed his narrative progress. My role was not to judge. Rather, it was to share his reflections and ask more questions. The blue linen notebook became the secure container in which he could create and situate his narrative. It was the place in which he could imagine and explore his possibilities. It provided the space for us to be "in" the succession experience together, as well as to be "on" it. And, it was the place in which he could make sense of his world.

RS's everyday coping with his succession was influenced and shaped by the preconceptions he brought to it and into his notebook. Once there, once experienced, and then reflected upon, these formed another set of preconceptions that he brought to the next stage of his journey. This is dynamic in its relationship. The part cannot be separated from the whole, nor the whole from the part. Drawing on Heidegger's hermeneutic circle (1953, 2010), one is in relationship with a part and with a whole at the same time. Our interpretation of the whole is influenced by what we bring to it from our experience and interpretation of the part.

Figure 6.6 illustrates this dynamic relationship (in a static form):

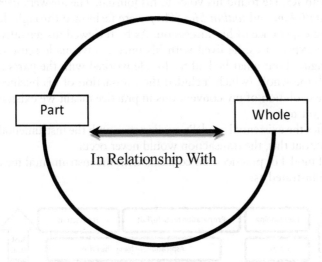

Figure 6.6 The hermeneutic circle – following Heidegger

Journaling allowed RS to reflect on his feelings about disruptive change and uncertainty. It gave him a voice with which he spoke to himself (first) and to others (second) about reframing himself and his world. It invited RS to be in relationship with the parts and the whole of his succession. Through journaling, he found ways of everyday coping with the uncertainty of his succession.

Locke and Weinberger (2011) speak to this in describing what it means existentially to be coping with uncertainty and contingency and finding ways, in ourselves, (not instrumentally) to deal with that:

> Look, we'd like to derive twelve happy instructions from the wash of ideas swirling around us . . .

> But, it doesn't work that way. This is an existential moment. It's characterized by uncertainty, the dissolving of the normal ways of settling uncertainties, the evaporation of the memory of what certainty was once like. In times like this, we all have an impulse to find something stable and cling to it, but then we'd miss the moment entirely. There isn't a list of things you can do to work the whirlwind. The desire to have such a list betrays the moment.

> There may not be twelve or five or twenty things you can do, but there are ten thousand. The trick is, you have to figure out what they are. They have to come from you. They have to be your words, your moves, your authentic voice.

> (2011, p. 243)

And so it was with RS. He found his voice in his journal. The answers *were* his. They were *with him* and *within him*. They were fashioned through the existentially lived experience of his succession. As he reviewed his narrative and his reflected experiences, he lived with his uncertainty, made sense of his world, and figured out what he had to do. He worked with the parts in relationship with the whole (which included the transaction of his business merger). And the evolution of my conventions in practice meant we existentially shared his journey.

This exemplifies the existential model's co-existence with the instrumental, technocratic. Without this, the transaction would never occur.

An existential model of practice that cohabits with the instrumental technocratic can be illustrated as:

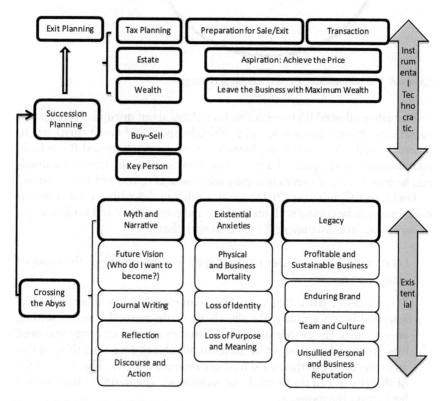

Figure 6.7 An Existential Model of Succession – Co-existing with the Instrumental Technocratic

This diagram illustrates the extent to which my model of practice has evolved. Whilst it is not linear, it creates a pathway from the existential to the instrumental technocratic. It accommodates both dimensions: the existential and the instrumental technocratic.

RS's moment of disruption when signing the contract emerged because he was thrown by the unexpected feeling of loss and grief for the business he was leaving. This feeling was a part that was resolved when he resumed his relationship with the whole: the narrative, imaginings, and possibilities he had created in the notebook.

Being *in* that moment of disturbance was also important for me. I had a felt sense of validation. I now had affirmation that the decision to shift from the instrumental technocratic to the existential felt right.

If, at the lawyer's office, we had defaulted to the instrumentally technocratic, RS may have walked away. In that case, the richness of his future-based narrative and the compass for his direction would have been lost. Instead, we both travelled an existential pathway.

Since then, RS has enjoyed his mentoring role. His financial reward has been significant. His sense of purpose and meaning in his life has been renewed. He is playing tennis (not golf!). He has a new circle of friends. His legacy is secure. His narrative is being acted out. And RS and I are friends.

The evolution of my conventions in practice has opened a pathway on which succession clients travel from their life-world of the "now" to their life-world of the "future" – from being *in* their business to being *out* of their business. Together we build – plank-by-plank – a bridge across the abyss.

I help them broaden their horizon to include the ends of succession, to understand and work with the relationship between means and ends and ends and means, and to stay in touch with the whole. This helps open up the space in which they discover meaning (their "will to meaning") in their succession journey. It enables them to endure the discomfort and disruptions of succession. It brings to mind Frankl's (1946, 1959) observation that "he who understands the why to live for can bear almost any how".

I notice that they elevate their level of engagement whilst further solving their succession dilemma.

The succession experience I have shared here about RS shows shifts in my conventions of practice. Initially, the *modus operandi* of my practice followed instrumental technocratic models.

Their legitimacy is not questioned. They provide a skeleton for the financial–legal–resource-based solutions that enable the transfer of ownership and/or management of a business into the hands of the next generation.

However, they are limited when confronted by the disruption of existential anxieties of stakeholders. An existential practice works with disruption and cohabits with the instrumental technocratic.

I have shifted my practice by being-in-practice. With succession clients, I have traversed the Sartrean abyss. Importantly, new clients bring their own new abyss whose crossing requires the painstaking building of a new existential bridge. With each new abyss comes a new disruption. This means the shifts in my conventions of practice remain a work-in-progress.

Thus, the evolution of my practice is incomplete. I continue to find fascinating the extent to which succession is influenced and shaped by fundamental, existential concerns. Attunement to them is a key attribute of an existential succession practitioner. That does not come easily. It opens up possibilities for practitioner education.

Existential conventions create barriers to entry for practitioners new to this space. To what should a practitioner in this space be open? They should listen – in Gendlin's interpretive, mirroring, non-judgmental way. They should embrace the existential conventions of practice of other disciplines such as nursing and teaching where existential and reflective practices are well known and accepted. Existential practitioners need courage to work with disruption, in a way suggested by Segal, that permits them to rethink, critique, and reinvent their conventions of practice.

The shifts and transformations in my models of practice have followed what Spinosa et al. called *cross-appropriation* – the bringing of different practices into contexts which could not generate them, but in which they are useful (1997, p. 4). Thus, I have cross-appropriated philosophical practices into the context of succession. And, in so doing, I have developed conventions of practice that might lead to meaningful historical change (Spinosa et al. 1997, p. 28).

I remain greatly curious about the narrowed horizon of other succession disciplines (including law, accounting, and financial planning) and the closed-ness of mind that their practitioners bring to anything other than their familiar models and conventions of practice. A question for future research is: what might allow these practitioners to open up to the possibilities of appreciating and engaging the ontological skill of disclosing new ways of being (Spinosa et al. 1997, p. 1).

This notion challenges and invites banks and the major wealth management, legal, and accounting firms to experiment by broadening their succession practices and advisory horizons beyond their familiar and comfortable. Future research might look into the limitations of disciplinary horizons and the organizational, social, and structural impediments to experimentation with conventions of practice in those organizations – as they and their clients would benefit most.

The dynamics and circularity of an existential hermeneutic approach to succession practice raises other questions for future research: (i) what room is there in the professional education of lawyers, accountants, and others for their immersion in existential practice; and what form would that take? And (ii) how and why could a model of existential hermeneutic "consulting" be scaled and extended into other consulting and advisory domains: for example, the field of mergers-and-acquisitions?

Bringing philosophy-as-practice into the conventions of business is an excitingly privileged opportunity. If we think about it too much, we will never jump the abyss.

References

Aristotle, 1975, *The Nicomachean ethics*, D.Reidel, Boston.

Barrett, R and Dunemann, M, 2004a, *Business Transitions – Linchpin Group Australia's Succession Planning Program – A Report*, Family and Small Business Research Unit, Faculty of Business and Economics, Monash University, Melbourne.

Barrett, R and Dunemann, M, 2004b, *Family Business and Succession Planning – A Review of the Literature*, FSBRU, Faculty of Economics, Monash University on behalf of The Linchpin Group Australia; accessed on 3 March 2009: http://www.buseco.monash.edu.au.simsrad.net.ocs.mq.edu.au/units/fsbru/fbsp-fsbru-report.pdf, Melbourne.

Baù, M, Hellerstedt, K, Nordqvist, M and Wennberg, K, 2013, 'Succession in Family Firms', in RL Sorenson, A Yu, KH Brigham and GT Lumpkin (eds), *The Landscape of Family Business*, Edward Elgar, Cheltenham, UK.

Beckhard, R and Burke, W, 1983, 'Preface', *Organizational Dynamics*, vol. 12, no. 1, p. 12.

Bryld, E, 2000, 'The technocratic discourse: Technical means to political problems', *Development in Practice*, vol. 10, no. 5, pp. 700–5.

Burke, F, 2003, 'Effective SME Family Business Succession Strategies', paper presented to the International Council for Small Business, 48th World Conference.

Carney, M and Jaskiewicz, P, 2014, 'Six Books That Have Shaped the Landscape of Family Business Scholarship', *Academy of Management Learning & Education*, p. amle. 2014.0260.

Combs, G and Freedman, J, 1996, *Narrative Therapy: The Social Construction of Preferred Realities*, Norton, New York.

CPA, 2004, *Small Business Succession and Exits*, CPA Australia, Melbourne.

Day, J, n.d., *Controlled Succession Planning*, The Kenneths Group, Melbourne.

Dreyfus, HL, 1991, *Being in the World – A Commentary on Heidegger's Being and Time, Division 1*, The MIT Press, Cambridge, MA.

Dreyfus, HL and Wrathall, MA (eds), 2005, 2007, *A Companion to Heidegger*, Blackwell Companions to Philosophy, Blackwell Publishing, Oxford.

Dyck, B, Mauws, M, Starke, F and Mischke, G, 2002, 'Passing the baton: The importance of sequence, timing, technique and communication in executive succession', *Journal of Business Venturing*, vol. 17, no. 2, p. 159.

Epston, D and White, M, 1990, *Narrative Means to Therapeutic Ends*, Norton, New York.

Fox, M, Nilakant, V and Hamilton, RT, 1996, 'Managing succession in family-owned businesses', *International Small Business Journal*, vol. 15, no. 1, pp. 15–25.

Frankl, V, 1946, 1959, *Man's Search for Meaning*, Rider, London.

Gadamer, H-G, 1980, *Dialogue and Dialectic: Eight Hermeneutical Studies on Plato*, Yale University Press, New Haven.

Gadamer, H-G, 1989, *Truth and Method* 2nd rev edn, Continuum, New York.

Geertz, C, 1973, *The Interpretation of Cultures*, Basic Books, New York.

Gendlin, ET, 1996, *Focusing-Oriented Psychotherapy – A Manual of the Experiential Method*, The Guildford Press, New York.

Glassop, L, Hagel, P and Waddell, D, 2006, *KPMG and Family Business Australia – Survey of Family Business Needs 2006*, KPMG, Melbourne.

Glassop, L, Hagel, P and Waddell, D, 2007, *KPMG and Family Business Australia – Survey of Family Business Needs 2007*, KPMG, Melbourne.

Glassop, L, Hagel, P and Waddell, D, 2008, *KPMG and Family Business Australia – Survey of Family Businesses 2008*, KPMG, Melbourne.

Glassop, L, Ho, YC and Waddell, D, 2005, *KPMG and Family Business Australia – Survey of Family Business Needs – A Synopsis*, KPMG, Melbourne.

Hamilton, L, 2003, 'SMES Succession Planning: Its Pros and Cons, a Survival Process?', paper presented to the International Council for Small Business, 48th World Conference, Belfast, UK.

Handler, WC, 1994, 'Succession in family business: A review of the research', *Family Business Review*, vol. 7, no. 2, pp. 133–57.

Heidegger, M, 1953, 2010, *Being and Time*, State University of New York, Albany, NY.

Heidegger, M, 1985, *History of the Concept of Time*, Indiana University Press, Bloomington, IN.

Heidegger, M, 1997, 2001, *Zollikon Seminars*, Northwestern University Press, Evanston, IL.

Holland, C, 2008, *The Art of Business Succession: Who Will Fill Your Shoes?*, John Wiley, Sydney.

Holman Jones, S, Adams, T and Ellis, C, 2013, 'Introduction: Coming to Know Autoethnography as More than a Method', in S Holman Jones, T Adams and C Ellis (eds), *Handbook of Autoethnography*, Left Coast Press, Walnut Creek, CA.

Hovey, W, 2014a, *Figure 6.2: Instrumental Succession as a Financial-based Process*, Linchpin Succession Management, Sydney.

Hovey, W, 2014b, *Figure 6.3: Instrumental Succession Combining Financial Outgcomes with Owner Preparation*, Linchpin Succession Management, Sydney.

Hovey, W, 2014c, *Figure 6.4: An Instrumental Succession Model Combining Financial, Owner, Successor and Transaction*, Linchpin Succession Management, Sydney.

Hovey, W, 2014d, *Figure 6.7: An Existential Model of Succession – Co-existing with the Instrumental Technocratic*, Linchpin Succession Management, Sydney.

Hovey, W, 2015a, *Figure 6.1: The Relationship Between The Instrumental and the Technocratic*, Linchpin Succession Management, Sydney.

Hovey, W, 2015b, *Figure 6.5: Relational Convenstions of Practice*, Linchpin Succession Management, Sydney.

Ip, B and Jacobs, G, 2006, 'Business succession planning: a review of the evidence', *Journal of Small Business and Enterprise Development*, vol. 13, no. 3, pp. 326–50.

Janesick, VJ, 1998, 'Journal Writing as a Qualitative Research Technique: History, Issues, and Reflections', paper presented to Annual Meeting of the American Educational Research Association, San Diego, CA.

Kierkegaard, S, 1944, *The Concept of Dread*, Princeton University Press, Princeton, NJ.

Kierkegaard, S, 1978, *Søren Kierkegaard's Journals and Papers*, vol. 5, Indiana University Press, Bloomington, IN.

Kierkegaard, S, 2000, *The Essential Kierkegaard*, Princeton University Press, Princeton, NJ.

Kirschner, S and Kirschner, D, 2000, 'Succession Planning in the Family-Owned Firm: Psycholegal Concerns', in F Kaslow (ed.), *Handbook of Couple and Family Forensics: A Sourcebook for Mental Health and Legal Practitioners*, John Wiley and Sons, New York, p. 336.

Le Breton-Miller, L, Miller, D, and Steier, LP, 2004, 'Toward an integrative model of effective FOB succession', *Entrepreneurship Theory and Practice*, vol. 28, no. 4, pp. 305–28.

Locke, C and Weinberger, D, 2011, *The Cluetrain Manifesto – The End of Business As Usual*, 10th Anniversary Edition edn, Basic Books, New York.

May, R, 1950, *The Meaning of Anxiety*, Norton, New York.

May, R, 1991, *The Cry For Myth*, WW Norton, New York.

May, R, 1994, *The Discovery of Being*, WW Norton, New York.

May, R, 2009, *Man's Search For Himself*, Norton, New York.

Morgan, A, 2000, *What is Narrative Thereapy?*, Dulwich Centre; accessed on 28 March 2014: http://www.dulwichcentre.com.au/what-is-narrative-therapy. html%3E.

Pendlebury, S, 1990, 'Practical arguments and situational appreciation in teaching', *Educational Theory*, vol. 40, no. 2, pp. 171–9.

Popovic, N, 2002, 'Existential anxiety and existential joy', *Practical Philosophy*, no. Autumn, pp. 32–9.

Poza, EJ, 2010, *Family Business*, 3rd edn, South-Western CENGAGE Learning, Mason, OH.

Progoff, I, 1975, *At a Journal Workshop*, Dialogue House, New York.

Sartre, J-P, 1938, 2010, *Nausea*, Penguin, Melbourne.

Sartre, J-P, 1947, *Existentialism*, New York: Philosophical Library.

Sartre, J-P, 1948, 1973, *Existentialism and Humanism*, Methuen, London.

Sartre, J-P, 2003, *Being and Nothingness*, Routledge, London.

Segal, S, 2015, *Management Practice and Creative Destruction*, Ashgate Gower, Farnham.

Sharma, P, Chrisman, JJ and Chua, JH, 2003, 'Predictors of satisfaction with the succession process in family firms', *Journal of Business Venturing*, vol. 18, no. 5, pp. 667–87.

Sharma, P, Chua, JH and Chrisman, JJ, 2000, 'Perceptions about the extent of succession planning in Canadian family firms', *Revue Canadienne des Sciences de l'Administration*, vol. 17, no. 3, pp. 233–44.

Smyrnios, K and Dana, L, 2006, *The MGI Family and Private Business Survey 2006*, RMIT, Melbourne.

Spinosa, C, Flores, F and Dreyfus, HL, 1997, *Disclosing New Worlds: Entrepreneurship, Democratic Action, and the Cuiltivationof Solidarity*, The MIT Press, Cambridge, MA.

van Deurzen-Smith, E, 1988, *Existential Counselling in Practice*, SAGE Publications, London.

White, M, 1997, ''The culture of professional disciplines', in *Narratives of Therapists' Lives*, Dulwich Centre Publications, Adelaide.

Yalom, ID, 1980, *Existential Psychotherapy*, Basic Books, New York.

Chapter 7

Midrash Methodology

Devorah Wainer

'Look!' he said to me. 'Look . . . here . . . the marks from the torture', he said, lifting his shirt, turning to show front and back.

I panic. I am trapped. I have to look. To see. To witness.

I have seen torture marks on others before now.

'Please God, don't let me recoil; please give me the strength to cope with this sighting'.

What is the appropriate response? I never know. Frequency hasn't immunized my horror. I am now one foot away, even less, from the site of such unforgiveable, unjustifiable, unwarranted, reprehensible disfigurement.

Even as I write now, telling this story, while so clearly picturing, re-experiencing, almost re-locating myself back there, I see the glistening newly erected, additional fences and wires at Villawood Detention Centre. Patches of brown dust, like a patchy skin disease, compete with the pathetic excuse for grass in the visitors' yard, the people dotted around each with their own cultural food smells wafting unbidden and definitely unwanted into the mix . . . The surveillance apparatus, the guards . . . (from Hineni)

(Wainer, 2015)

The gold standard for academic research methods, up to a decade ago, held that a researcher is able to produce a knowable reality, separate from the researcher. The methodology depicted in this chapter overturns that academic disjunction between theory and practice. This chapter is about a new genre of research methodology well suited to twenty-first century research that seeks to create critical awareness; raise consciousness; challenge dominant ideologies and build coalitions across groups. By offering holistic and integral approaches to research, by acknowledging and including the relationship of the researcher to her research environment, and to her work per se, the methodology described and narrated here fits snugly with a researcher who is living the experiences that she is researching.

Such work includes the self, thereby bringing transparency with a dignified presence of the researcher–author who writes in a style that can be creative, poetic and descriptive as it layers and nests iterative cycles of writing, reflecting and analysing. The researcher approaches the subject – an individual being who is unique – seeking to find out who is speaking and why, rather than merely to know what is said (Levinas, 1961).

I am one of Leavy's 'others' (Leavy, 2009) who eschews positivism, refusing traditional social science or humanities methodologies that risk objectifying the very subjects on whose behalf they appear to be advocating. I sought a method suited to the lived-life and the told-story.

My academic field of research is with asylum-seeking refugees within the contexts of International Human Rights, Australian detention systems and border crossings, and my sensitivities to methodology originate with my experiences and relationships behind the wire – inside Villawood Detention Centre. I would not further (in addition to incarceration) silence and invisibilise the detainees by usurping their agency, representation and voice. Instead my writing would orient the reader towards:

> [H]earkening to the human voice, where it speaks forth unfalsified, and replying to it, this above all is needed today. This voice must not only be listened to, it must be answered and led out of the lonely monologue into the awakening dialogue of the peoples.
>
> (Kepnes, 1992)

I was catapulting towards a methodology that draws on the muscle of a reflexive self, creativity and the ability to dream new futures – the Midrash Methodology.

Writing Midrash

> At the intersection of lived-lives and told-stories, the storied nature of human experience is research that does not begin conceptually with a theoretically proposed design and methodology. At the intersection of telling, re-telling and living, the storied research explores serious issues
>
> (Wainer, 2015)

Midrash means exposition, investigation or searching. Similarly phenomenology is a research orientation providing rich insights into the every day world of humans. Phenomenological research can also be approached as hermeneutical research. Hermeneutical studies, according to Becker, reads texts interpretatively, and witnesses life-events, reframing and re-languaging them. 'Hermenutic work is dynamic, creative and open-ended' (Becker, 1992).

In turn, midrash has the power to moderate a story or a conception that is in danger of becoming fixed – rigid and bound. The hermeneutics of phenomenology and midrash converge in the Midrash Methodology.

Alternate to a theoretical conception, personal experiences that trouble or puzzle a researcher (Reinharz, 1992) can be the starting point of an inquiry. A disruption in my life prompted a trajectory of questioning, self-reflexivity and writing that became social research. Impelled by my visits to asylum-seekers indefinitely incarcerated in an Australian detention centre – Villawood Detention Centre – I began writing midrashim.[1] During the first month of those visits, as I exited the detention centre I felt my head spinning and I vomited. I was discombobulating. Never previously having encountered prison institutions, apparatchik and systems, I had absolutely no idea what was happening to me during and at the end of each visit. To make sense of such powerfully confusing experiences, and to understand why despite them I continued returning to the detention centres, I began writing multilayered, meditative, poetic, self-reflexive midrashim.

A Tension Awakened (from the Midrash Cherry Ripe)

As I write I recall my anger at and loathing for the guard and the detention-prison system. I feel the tension constricting my neck and, as if straining backwards, reminding me of my reaction that day. Before I began writing this story I hadn't noticed the tension in my shoulders, neck and thighs. Have I been living with these tense muscles? Have they just knotted up now? Or is this a cellular memory of my tension in those days now activated with the writing of the story? My attention is on my tense thighs. The standing in the queue for too long, again and again each visit, accumulating-the-tension thighs. In those days it was easy to imagine the tense thighs were due to the standing.

Together with the thighs my neck and shoulders are also screaming at me with the burning, ripping, tightening of muscles that never completely relax. As if they have lost their intelligence or the know-how of 'relax'. Does my body need some let-go-and-relax nous?

What about the people detained, existing year upon year, in an unrelenting state of tension? Unable to sleep at night due to the fear, anxiety and terror related to apparently unresolvable and indefinite detention. Additionally people detained told me they also suffered from memories of torture and trauma that amplified when they closed their eyes at night. Memories that precluded sleep, as did the ever-present deep grieving for their losses – family, friends, freedom. Dropping into a fitful sleep as dawn approached, no exercise for the 3, 4, 5 years of incarceration, produced

---

1   Midrashim is the plural of Midrash.

aching bodies that moved about like partially stooped, ponderous old men in pain. Shuffling about, their watery bodies seemed not to breathe, as if halting the breath would block at their nostrils the acrid smell of the pervasive tension filling the air in the Villawood Detention Centre.

Now it is so blindingly obvious to me that the accumulation of tension started on the first day I visited Villawood.

My attention was awakened to a tension awakened . . .

(Wainer, 2015)

Writing in a style that includes reflexive questions to and of the self, I began opening up the phenomenology of living relations and shared situations behind the wire, inside Australian detention centres. Wilcke (2006) affirms the goal of phenomenology is to reveal meaning by paying attention to that which has been so taken for granted that it has not been questioned, thus seeking a deeper understanding of human experience by rediscovering it and opening it up. Very few in Australia, and no-one in the media, seemed to pay attention to the daily lives passing hour by hour, year by year, of those people incarcerated in the detention centres.

The stories I was writing were unveiling layers of description and inter-pretation of events and relationships behind the wire. They were attesting to a hitherto unknown world of rich lived relationships and caring shared situations behind the wire. Political and media reporting on people seeking asylum was determined to depersonalise and disembody them. As I wrote about my experiences of dialogical relating behind the wire, I was unwit-tingly enlivening, embodying and revealing the lived-lives of asylum-seekers within the detention regime.

A good [phenomenological] description that constitutes the essence of something is construed so that the structure of a lived experience is revealed to us in such a fashion that we are now able to grasp the nature and significance of this experience in a hitherto unseen way.

(Van Manen, 1990)

Our experiences can be best understood through stories we tell of that experience. To understand the life world we need to explore the stories people tell of their experiences.

(Kafle, 2011)

The Inquiry Process Itself is Storied

I continued living the experiences about which I wrote. Initially I went into the detention centres to visit. When I discovered a young Iraqi man soon due for his court appearance who was completely unprepared and anxious, I became more involved. After he received refugee status, a visa and left

Villawood Detention Centre I began advocating for the next person. And so it went person after person. During my visits, sometimes thrice weekly, I encountered people and events that hitherto were unknown to me – and remain unknown to the general Australian public. As I wrote questions bubbled up in me, eventually demanding attention. Soon I began drawing on felt-memories to enhance a deeper understanding of my experiences behind the wire in Villawood Detention Centre.[2]

Attention Awakened (from the Midrash Cherry Ripe)

It was my tense body that came to mind . . .

Leaving Villawood Detention Centre, I was disquieted. Why had I rejected so callously and offhandedly the love token? Half consciously, and quickly, before the self-reflexive musing could progress, I closed off the felt-thought that was already an ache. The ache that already was developing into a pain, a floating intermittent, empty pain. The pain detained. The ache generalised alongside other wounds.

Maya Angelou writes that history, despite its wrenching pain, cannot be unlived and, if faced with courage, need not be lived again. When pausing to reflect upon that summer's day, inside Villawood Detention Centre, I noticed my attention shift subtly from the non-invasive musing of the mind to a knot locked in my belly. And then I notice the move of the knot to my throat, too. There – simultaneously in the belly and the throat – the knot revealed itself to me. Paying attention to the feeling of tightness in my gut opened the recognition of the constriction in my throat. Recognition that this knot in the belly and the constriction in the throat are apparently connected: an unknown stranger dwelling within. A hitherto invisibilised part. Now it moves to arrive in my consciousness – locates . . . places . . . speaks . . . calls . . . asking to be seen and recognised. Unconsciously, I had thought I could control body pain by sublimation, by denial – by locking it away . . .

Not a new sensation, not a new pain, instead now, newly attended.

Is this a call for the courage of which Angelou writes? The courage to face not the thought-memory; the courage to face the felt-memory. In his article 'Venturing Past Psychic Numbing: Facing the Issues', psycho-analyst Robert Gregory writes that there is an almost gravitational pull towards putting out of mind unpleasant facts. Quoting Daniel Goleman, Gregory (2003) continues, 'We tune out, we turn away, we avoid. Finally we forget, and forget we have forgotten. A lacuna hides the harsh truth'.

---

2   Villawood Detention Centre is written in full to remain true to the way detainees used it in full.

While I hid the 'harsh truth' from myself, I othered this part of the story together with the meaning that is interwoven with experience. Only by inquiring could I discover the meaning that I gave to that specific experience. Only by engaging with the stranger within could I relax and release the knot in the belly and the constricted throat.

(Wainer, 2015)

Principles for Writing Midrash

My dialogical relating with the detainees compelled me to avoid being the agent for their experiences. The writing had to reveal the essence and texture of the experience and sensitively place them within the complexity of the whole environment without totalising or flattening experiences and relationships. This required me to write with a voice other than the reporting style typical of a traditional researcher.

Four principles were set for writing the midrashim:

1   An ethical framing wherein I could ground the self as well as the other as sacred.
2   To write about them in a style that could (re)cognise their dignity.
3   To wrap the incarcerated asylum-seekers in writing that is aesthetic and multi-sensorial.
4   For the sake of the reader (and my aesthetic appreciation), to write beautifully.

Initially I began writing to address my questions, to make sense of new experiences and emotions, incorporating the four principles. Equally as I reflected on each midrash I noticed that if my experiences are transposed to a detainees experience like Mohammed's or Ahmed's, a research pathway to the detainee's experience inside[3] was opened.

> A phenomenological description is always one interpretation, and no single interpretation of human experience will ever exhaust the possibility of yet another complementary, or even potentially richer or deep description.
>
> (Van Manen, 1990)

The two excerpts, *Attention awakened* and *A tension awakened* from the midrash Cherry Ripe (Wainer, 2015) show how subsequent to the author's

---

3   *Inside* is typical lexicon of prisoners. So too the detainees used prison language when speaking about inside the detention centre.

reflections on the tension she feels in her body, she finds 'memories' that paradoxically she never thought or felt before. Personal felt-memories open up the space to consider, by association, the possible experiences of the detainees. Such insights engendered further questions. They show a pathway specifically from my unconsciously numbed self and suppressed pain to explicating how much more so did the detainees lock parts of their experiences away, become numb and ill, while inside Villawood Detention Centre?

> 19:00. Visiting time is over and it is time to leave the visitors yard of surveillance at Villawood Detention Centre.
>
> The ritual hugs of the dead. Today both of us are dead. Leaving time always triggers his transformation back into the bent old man. His hands like claws that cannot really take hold of the wire fencing. Arms disappear. I see only the numbness-deadening, receding eyes staring alternately at the ground and then at me as I pass through the first unlock-and-lock gate. Like a scarecrow unable to stand upright, he flops even lower, his arms now visible as if they have re-joined his hands. Using the wire fencing, he holds himself up. I turn, as I always turn for a last glance, to see him before the next unlock and step into the blue infra-light vacuum chamber. I don't care about the unlocking-locking and more unlocking-locking. Each rattle of keys, the slam of gates, odours of guards, guards' uniforms, muted words of other departing visitors, take me further and further from my known self. Simultaneously deceiving and slowly numbing myself, I rationalise: 'Of course I can't FEEL this farewelling week after week, year after year. I would become immobilised with the anguish of seeing him re-collapsed into the unwelcome detainee, as I walk away to the Sydney bush and beaches, the laughter and love of my family'. I add to and shift my story, thereby making it more comfortable to sensibilities, further inducing an othered numbness that becomes corporealised pain while locked within. Only years later will it be recognised, welcomed and released.
>
> Then I am 'outside' and in my car.
>
> (from Cherry Ripe)
(Wainer, 2015)

I thought I could forget in-between each visit as I categorised and locked those people and events away. I couldn't. Why was I so uncomfortable? What really bothered me?

Sequencing

Writing first, before reading too much or analysing is crucial. The researcher–author consciously avoids introjecting into the midrashim what she thinks the midrashim might be telling her. Importantly a few midrashim must be written before turning to the literature as the researcher–author needs to avoid writing the midrashim to fit any pre-conceived literary frameworks. After writing them the researcher asks: What are the midrashim telling me?

I actually had written Hineni[4] before Cherry Ripe. But only after writing Cherry Ripe, did I notice that 'numbing' was a theme repeating itself in both midrashim.

> I cant even recall how I felt at that moment! Dare I even admit this to be so? I feel shame that after one and half years I have no felt-memory. Visual memory there is. I recall what Sara wore. I recall how Ahmed hovered – watching – yet remaining incognito. Yet what did I feel when holding this traumatized and terrified, clinging and crying, no long a stranger to me, young woman. Sara was the same age as my daughter. What causes this loss of feeling? Did I feel then? And only now, while writing, I don't feel, or can't recall what I felt? Was it the numbing again?
>
> (from Hineni)
> (Wainer, 2015)

How can we know *their experiences* inside, indefinitely detained, existing year upon year, in an unrelenting state of tension? At that time 95–99 per cent of all detainees were released as genuine refugees and are today citizens. They and their families will be our neighbours, teachers, husbands, community and politicians. It is my contention that to know their history is more than of archival importance. Yet research was (and is) banned inside a detention centre. What can be described of their experiential meanings they lived as they lived them? The questions I am asking are raised to engage the reader with the topic, situation, people – the text. Midrashic questions are not Socratic. Midrash questions are dialogic – raised to engage the reader with the text. They are questions of relationship, interpretation and meaning rather than timelines, numbers and facts.

The researcher–author is requesting the reader to engage with her text and to consider the life-worlds of the subjects by association with her told-stories. If the author experiences for example physical tension, and numbing, that she has ignored, denied or suppressed and 'then forgotten', until she has the opportunity to write, how much more so would the state of ongoing incarceration effect asylum-seekers? They come into detention already traumatised and may never have the opportunity or method to face and release such suppressed or denied experienced-memories. The goal of the Midrash Methodology is to invite the reader to enter the world that the texts discloses

---

4 Hineni literally means 'Here I am'. It is more than a physical placement and presence. Hineni is also to show up as a full and open being.

and to dialogue with it themselves. At the intersection of the midrash, the author–researcher and the listener is interpretation.

Interpretation

Locked in that prison, Villawood Detention Centre, for almost four years when this excerpt of which I write took place, Rami the detainee is invisible, unknown to the world outside. He is the one locked up and living according to externally imposed rigid institutional rules. Yet in the cameo *Once upon a Rainy Day*, Rami is the actor who impossibly finds and arranges the chairs to create a more comfortable space for Devorah. He makes Devorah laugh. He has internal freedom and spaciousness. I, Devorah, was frozen and rigid in a suppressed rage from the treatment of the guards processing me. I was numb with my inability to cope being inside, when greeting the detainee I knew – Nawu. Devorah invisibilised herself. Rami showed up.

Once Upon a Rainy Day (from Cherry Ripe)

Today I am visiting Rami. Where is he? I make my way past Nawu who rises to greet me, kissing both cheeks. A faint glimmer of life flickers in his eyes only momentarily and then he sits again. I nod silent greetings to his visitors, some of whom I know; others I recognise as Regulars. All the while my eyes darting: Where is Rami?

'How you, Nawu?'

'Good, good – thank you. Fine'.

Not me, I remember thinking, not me. I have only had the past 10 minutes of lost independence, icily ripped from me by the prison guards, and I am raging. I feel lost. How can you say fine, Nawu? I think. What is fine?

In the remembering now, I am also wondering who was more lost then. Was Nawu lost to his free self, for the years of denial of freedom and of individuality? Or was I, because of the immediacy of my experience?

'How you, Devorah?'

'Thank God, Nawu. Thank God', I reply as the customary greeting, the greeting of his custom, culture and country, begins it's turn-taking dance. I had learnt to say 'Thank God' in this dance from the detainees I visit.

WHY do I ask about his family from whom he is separated? It is polite to ask. I am recognising he has a family. I ask for the same reason I bother about my appearance. And so the greetings continue. He inquires about my children, I about his. All the while my eyes darting, looking for Rami.

I'm feeling prickly. All sorts of people – asylum seekers, visa over-stayers due for impending deportation, convicted criminals without visas – are packed tightly together under the only shelter from the rain in the visitors yard of surveillance in Villawood Detention Centre.

I'm panicking. I DON'T WANT to be here . . . WHERE is Rami?

At that moment an arm encircles my waist and I am turned around 180 degrees. Rami is there by my side. Saving me. But from what?

'Where the hell were you?' I hiss at him.

'There', he points. 'There. I didn't even see you arrive. I am so sorry. It's this crowd here. I didn't see you. So sorry. I'm so stupid – I didn't see you – I'm sorry . . . '

'Nawu said you went to your room', I accuse him.

Gently, quietly: 'No, I didn't'.

Rami performed the impossible. He created a space for just the two of us with the two chairs that he was guarding. Just two chairs for us. He knows I have a strong distaste for the crowding, the bodies, the smells, the sensations, the confusion under that sole, inadequate shelter on rainy days.

I breathe a sigh of relief. We sit opposite each other. Facing each other, knees touching, leaning forward on our white plastic bucket chairs. I look deeply into his eyes – and I settle. Looking into eyes is how I have learnt to know the answer to the unspoken question: 'How are you?'

Rami, permitting me to look silently into his eyes, is a gentle soul. A perceptive young man. He extends himself now – for me. He knows how to make me laugh. And does exactly this.

Here under the shelter, where visitors and people detained are squashed together on the white bucket chairs that leave no room to move freely from group to group; where bodies rub up against bodies in too close proximity; where the food smells attack all pervasively; the sky is dark, thick and brooding and the rain renders hearing almost impossible. It is the laughter that rises above the hushed sounds of people sharing conversation, couples' intimacies; English or French learners; babies crying; teenagers yelling and the slurping of noodle soups. The laughter is magnetic. Roles have been reversed: the inmate, my friend, has given me, a visitor from the free world, asylum from the harsh distressing environment.

(Wainer, 2015)

Only after writing two of the three midrashim I turned to literature as I began to signify and frame felt-thoughts about my experiences. Hoping for illumination I turned to Derrida, Buber, Agamben, Akhmatova, Arendt, Foucault, theatre, film and poetry, to make sense of my behaviour and emotional landscape that day, and generally. Theory helped me begin framing my understanding of life and events inside Villawood Detention Centre for the detained and the Australians who visited them. The narratives themselves were becoming disruptive spaces of dialogic relating. The writing was transforming into a research project and I served as my own exegete. The midrashim 'were already starting to become research literature per se' (Wainer, 2015).

The philosophy of Emmanuel Levinas, described as one of the greatest philosophers of the twentieth century, lifted the veils of my confusion. Shining a light on the phenomenology of alterity, Levinas' philosophy was already becoming the theoretical framework for my research.

An Other-centred Ethic

Unlike theoretical reasoning that aims for closure, bounds and fixes the Other, the ethical relationship is, as any relationship, open. The human I is not a unity closed upon itself, like the uniqueness of the atom, but rather an opening, that of responsibility, which is the true beginning of the human and, of spirituality.

(Levinas, 1984)

Ethically and aesthetically Levinas intersects with the values I set for my writing and my worldview. He was deeply concerned about ethical actions of response-ability. The ethics of which Levinas speaks is not 'a simple moralism of rules which decree what is virtuous. It is the original awakening of an I responsible for the other' (Ibid.). The 'original awakening' refers to an unbidden act of compassion to the Other, particularly the sick, the needy, the Stranger. The face of the Other speaks even if not a word is uttered. Importantly, responsiveness to the presence of the 'face' is an act, not a thought. 'The call which the face of the other man addresses to me . . . is the lived experience of authentic humanity' (Ibid.). In the face-to-face encounter we must listen with all of our being to ascertain *who* is communicating and *why*. Other-centred ethics invokes an awakening and emerging I – the self – who is responsible to the Other. Accordingly, Levinas' ethics is nonnormative and differs from normative ethics.

Martin Buber, a twentieth-century sociologist, writer of Chasidic tales and mystic declares that 'All real living is meeting' (Buber, 1958).

A Stranger cannot be known by thinking about him.[5] The consequence of which, according to Levinas, cruelly 'neutralises' him by stripping his unique

---

5   The masculine form is used in concurrence with the majority of detainees who were male.

character, his values and dreams, and denies him his own agency. Relating face to face behind the wire, in the visitor's yard of surveillance at Villawood Detention Centre stands in stark contrast to the political and media commentary that spurns, abandons and neutralises the asylum-seeker, despite never having met one. Response-ability is relating in an encounter *with* the unique *Other*.

In terms of an ethics of response-ability I found myself lacking on that rainy day in the Cherry Ripe midrash in the way I responded to Rami's token of love, affection or friendship. A few visits earlier he told me in the context of his four years' incarceration, 'You are my whole family: My mother, father, sisters, brothers, aunts, uncles, cousins'. So why did I recoil from his token?

> As others choose their chocolates from Rami's box of sweets, he moves even closer to me. His deep-brown eyes soft pools now. He opens his palm towards me. In it lies on red-wrapped Cherry Ripe. 'This is for YOU', he gently mouths.
>
> This is his love wrapped in bright red cellophane. The love for which he is truly yearning. More than one dozen red roses of a free man are offered to me.
>
> His palm open, my eyes somehow simultaneously on his palm and looking into his eyes, I take a breath. The only bit of red, wrapped around the chocolate, is the sacred offering, the sacred declaration of this moment. It is sacred, true to and pure within this moment.

And I reject it!

The moment I refused the Cherry Ripe I shifted from dialogical relating *with* to thinking *about*. No longer was I living Buber's injunction of 'real living'. I, Rami's 'whole family' failed – to meet – him. I fell short of the ethical act, refusing the 'awakened I' as I shifted my stance from relating *with* Rami – the opening human – to thinking *about* Rami – the detainee.

Putting it All Together

I began my doctoral research project believing that I would be writing about racism within the context of Australian multiculturalism. At that time, my professional role was senior director in the government. Life was good.

In my role as director, I proposed an ethical, fiscally responsible, whole-of-government project regarding a more dignified and respectful policy for receiving asylum-seeking refugees. Although highly commended, the timing was not quite right for such a project. Into the Minister's bottom draw it went. I was furious that the inhumane detention system was politically preferred. It was almost the turn of the century with the twenty-first century offering hope and a better world for all. Instead of staying with the anger that was born of my crushed hope for a more just policy, I decided to go inside, to visit, in my personal and private capacity – to meet the vilified and invisibilised asylum-seekers. I would learn more about these people who, without trial or conviction, are incarcerated indefinitely.

Inside detainees are treated like convicted criminals, invisibilised from the public eye and silenced consequential to the criminal–penal culture and systems into which they are thrust. In that space of indefinite incarceration they are more effectively cut off from the world of the living than if they were dead (Arendt, 1948). This deeply concerned me. Additionally, I was deeply bothered by the apparent absence of care or consciousness Australians had regarding the incarcerated asylum-seeking refugees. Why were the inhumane conditions of the detainees' daily lives behind the wire missing from the media and social discourse?

With that question in mind I changed the direction of my doctoral research. My lived experiences, my personal confusions, questions and searches for meaning initiated the doctoral thesis *Beyond the Wire: Levinas vis-à-vis Villawood* that went on to receive the most coveted academic award for the outstanding calibre of doctoral research. The Midrash Methodology satisfies the most rigorous of academic scrutiny, which includes this style of academic writing.

The multi-vocal, multi-sensorial midrashim that I had begun writing and the insights I embodied from the literature I was reading were midwifing the new research methodology. I wrote (re)presentations of that which I had experienced and witnessed behind the wire in the visitors' yard of surveillance in Villawood Detention Centre. Understanding the asylum-seeker in terms of the Other who I could never know, yet with whom I came face to face, I could write ethically and aesthetically about situations and people so totally foreign to me – the life and environment of incarceration.

Reflexively I noticed qualities in the midrashim like those discussed by Denzin and Lincoln (2003) who anticipated a method of research for the twenty-first century. They describe six moments in qualitative research during the years 1900–2000. Since the turn of the century, research entered into what they term the Seventh Moment – research concerned with moral discourse.

> We imagine a form of qualitative inquiry in the 21st century that is simultaneously minimal, existential, autoethnographic, vulnerable, performative, and critical. This form of inquiry erases traditional distinctions among epistemology, ethics, and aesthetics; nothing is value-free. It seeks to ground the self in a sense of the sacred, to connect the ethical, respectful self, dialogically to nature and the worldly environment
>
> (Denzin and Lincoln, 2003)

The midrashim take into account the impossibility of bearing witness (Agamben, 1998) and the concerns a researcher has for the agency and voice of the Other. Traditional boundaries between researcher, author, research subject and research environment disappear, as a midrashic fission actuates at the intersection of researcher as author, Other, text and world. The Midrash Methodology begins with one's lived experience and offers new pathways for knowledge creation.

Phase One

Midrashim are written as the first phase of the methodology. The experience when writing is of various states of rhythm, energy and flow[6] (Csikszentmihalyi, 2008). The following excerpt accounts for tension and despair due to what I thought was a writer's block without allowing myself to trust the unconscious self is the real genius as George Bernard Shaw asserts. Once I surrendered to the text – my unconscious – allowing the writing to asserted itself, I was astonished by the relevance and importance of the narrative.

The Windmills of My Mind:[7] My Story Becomes Midrash

January: I am writing as I sit cross-legged on my comfortable, new-ish, blue, modern-ish, minimalist-ish couch. Gentle cooking aromas, wafting through my open patio doors call my attention. Indian spices! I think I have smelt Indian food cooking for the past few days. 'Must have new neighbours'. Yet another floating thought passes through my mind. The mind that I think is concentrating on writing this story. The next thought pattern, linking in like a nested Russian doll, takes me to my recent trip to India. I am seeing those exquisite multicoloured saris in a blended image with the girl-woman, baby on hip, hands thrust begging into our little pfut-pfut cab. The smog-filled air smells are not yet familiar to me. Oil, kerosene, incense, goats, dung, human bodies. Low cloud at dusk seemingly responsible for their mingling into one aroma that I now label as Mumbai! Mount Abu was different, I muse. Subtract from Mumbai the densely packed numbers of people. Add space to the best of Mumbai; add Naki Lake and monkeys. Dogs, too!

With a jolt I realise I am not writing or concentrating on the story.

---

6 Flow is the sense of inspired freedom that comes when you lose yourself completely in an activity, allowing time, duty and worry to melt away. For writer's, words pour out in a continuous, creative stream.

7 'The Windmills of Your Mind'. Words & music by Alan & Marilyn Bergman & Michel Legrand (from the film *The Thomas Crown Affair*): 'Round, like a circle in a spiral / Like a wheel within a wheel./ Never ending or beginning, / On an ever-spinning wheel . . .'.

Is this avoidance? The past two weeks I have tried to write this story. Each time my keyboard fingers move in a saying of their own.

'What am I writing?' I ask myself with disdain. The pitch of my internal voice rising.

Ctrl S. Save.

Yet another version.

Diligently try again.

Day after day I observe this story, in varying versions, arriving of its own volition on the page that is my computer screen. After saving Cherry Ripe_vs5 on my seventh or eighth day of attempting to write the story I had planned, had intended to write, I give up – bereft!

'This is NOT what I am meant to write. WHY can't I write any more?' I agonise. The writing is the seeker of asylum. I am the politician saying,

'We don't want writing like this on the pages of our computer screen'.

I am the guard vigilantly taking muster regularly to check if the illegally arrived words are well detained and incarcerated; locked away from the other words that I have already sanctioned as valid and useful for this project.

The border guards of my mind expand their control, excising certain islands of thought as invalid for the Cherry Ripe story.

'Exercise! I am physically tight so obviously my mind is tight', I rationalise to myself. Dawning on me at that moment, as a huge revelation bringing immense relief, is the (in hindsight) illusion that I am taking control – that I am able to willfully control this writing project with the logical assessment:

'I need to exercise'.

The following day, fresh and enthusiastic, I sit down to write. And yet again – the same flotsam and jetsam of words and phrases that are strange to me arrive on the page that is my computer screen. Uninvited memory – sensations of that rainy day in Villawood Detention Centre invade and overwhelm my body. I look for . . . Music! 'Some agreeable-soothing-help-me-concentrate music to banish this unwanted sensate arrival', I muse as I turn my music collection. The tense, lactic-acid-locked-in muscles mixed together with the metallic, rancid-anxiety smells of Villawood Detention Centre are intolerable and must be banished.

The gorgeous clear blue skies terrorise my vision, and the ideal summer temperatures plague me. I hear the call 'go to the beach'; 'a swim will be delicious'; 'you need some exercise' (again!) (daily?); 'the sea will be perfect for the body today'.

Music! My defence against these unwelcome self-indulgent perhaps even self-sabotaging internal voices.

Searching through my CDs for the 'right music', unwittingly I encounter the CD that I often (read 'obsessively, always') played en route, driving to and from Villawood Detention Centre in the lived-time of this story.

I know that music generally touches me, my soul, so that I can access the topography of my corporealised pain, wherein lie the frozen and numb detained parts of myself. But I thought I was selecting 'concentration' music; help-me-focus-on-my-writing music. Almost not of my own voli-tion, I place that CD in the player.

Now, hearing the words of the songs that I played during those inter-minable drives, to and from Villawood Detention Centre, I begin to wonder: 'Was I numb then? Am I numb now? How numb am I?'

Possibly just numb enough to go through the wire again and again and again. Or, so numb that I don't even know how numb. . . .

'But tell me if you are coming tomorrow . . . ' Bocelli.

The healing, life-affirming tears flow. I am no longer the intelligent-in-control-of-my-writing doctoral student. As if claiming a lost part of myself – perhaps a new part of myself is expanding – no longer am I able to avoid scrutinising the representations that defy my presumptions of the story. These representations, of their own accord, consistently appear on the pages of my computer screen. And I concede.

(Wainer, 2015)

Transparency

Because the researcher is also the researched she reflects to understand the influences and worldviews that consciously and unconsciously come to bear on her work. All research is value-laden. Beyond the Wire includes a dia-grammatic figure to illustrate the possible influences such as an immigrant to Australia who felt strange and Other; a former activist against the unethi-cal South African apartheid regime who felt estranged and Othered from her country of birth; a former leader in multicultural New South Wales and a Jewish woman. As a researcher is not separate from her research, the Midrash Methodology requests researcher awareness and transparency by locating the self, the relevant influences that come to bear and one's world-view, within the research. Gadamer refers to fore-meanings as the means by which we orient ourselves to a topic and states.

The important thing is to be aware of one's own bias, so that the text can present itself in all its otherness and thus assert its own truth against one's own fore-meanings

(Gadamer, 1979)

Personal awareness and reflection underpin the Midrash Methodology. Possible influences and orientations must be shown at the beginning of a project for the reader to engage dialogically with an honest and transparent text. Thus my identity as an ex-South African, a Director in government, an advocate and visitor to Villawood Detention Centre and amongst others my spiritual inner-world all came to bear on the research albeit in different proportions. Equally so making visible my cultural heritage, education and personal life-experiences contribute to the reader's clarity about myself the researcher as participant and data source; myself the researcher as author and instrument.

Phase Two

The second phase of the Midrash Methodology requires the researcher to include insights that form a multilayered and multi-vocal weaving back and forth. The researcher validates the insights, themes or findings from the primary data – the midrashim – with secondary data. I call this the 'so what?' step. 'So what' if data or a motif is evidenced within the context of a midrash? Is it identifiable or supported elsewhere from other reliable, validated sources? Here follows an example 'so what' secondary data.

Every time I visit, I do my best to look good. The people detained see none other than their guards and visitors. What would they care how I look? Normally I have 'bad hair' days; 'don't know what to wear' days; 'Gee, don't I look good in that' days; or 'Who cares – no one will even notice' days. But never one of those days when visiting Villawood Detention Centre. Dressing well, looking good, was one small way I could show respect to the captives I visit. The non-verbal communication I attempt is 'You are special'; 'You are important to me'; 'You deserve a presentation of myself that is appropriate, considered and clear'. It seemed so important to always give that respect; that regard; that consideration – as if my thoughts, my appearance, could annul some of the vitriol poured on the detainees.

. . .

Then it was my turn to huddle under the narrow door lintel just before stepping through the entrance to the processing room.

'Two', the prison guards announce, glaring at the visitor who sought shelter by stepping 'out of turn' under the beam for cover. The briefly triumphant stance of upright spine and broad shoulders changes to droop as the visitor steps back, the one step necessary, to again be 'waiting in turn' in the rain, so that only the requisite 'Two' enter.

(Wainer, 2015)

Reading three unedited midrashim that I had written for *Beyond the Wire* I identified a theme relating to the visitors who stood for hours in the queues waiting to be processed by petulant, disparaging or abusive prison guards. Was there secondary data that would support the effect of the queuing and the prison culture on the visitor as already written in the midrashim? The integrity of the methodology requires the supporting evidence – secondary data – for an emerging theme from the midrashim – primary data – without rewriting any of the midrashim.

Already earlier in this chapter, reference to Maya Angelou and Goleman supports the theme of numbing as it shows up in the midrashim. What meaning can we make about the treatment of the queuing visitor in the midrashim? *Beyond the Wire* refers to two sources of supporting data. Anna Akhmatova's Requiem as well as The Affidavits of the Intake Service Center (ISC), which is a maximum-security facility for male offenders on Rhode Island. Under the heading *Disrespectful Treatment at the Intake Centre*, a mother reports her treatment by the guards. She also questions the suffering of the incarcerated 'by association' with her own experience. 'If I am made to feel this way, then what goes on behind closed bars?'

> I was visiting my son in intake in the summer of 2003. Upon passing through the metal detector it beeped. The man in front of me had on steel toe boots and a short spiked belt. He was asked to remove these items and allowed to put them back on. The reason the detector beeped after taking off my shoes was because of my underwire bra.
>
> I was asked to remove my bra as no wand to scan me was available. I was not allowed to put my bra back on and I only had a tee shirt on. I hadn't seen my son in quite some time due to an injury and being hospitalized. However I was allowed to go to the waiting area down stairs and await his visit.
>
> Each guard commented on how they liked my tee shirt. The tee shirt was plain white. It wasn't the tee shirt they were looking at. After sitting for 10 minutes I was told my son had lost his visit. Upon leaving the guards commented on the tee shirt again. My arms were across my chest. I was humiliated and I asked to see a female officer. They answered, 'We don't have any on duty'. I asked for the senior officer. They answered, 'He's in a meeting'.
>
> The guard who had me remove my bra was aware of my son losing his visit and seemed to enjoy my humility. I asked for his badge number

and name. He said, 'Don't catch cold now and laughed'. This was total discrimination. Needless to say I cried in the parking lot. I felt violated and it seemed like I was the prisoner. If I am made to feel this way, then what goes on behind closed bars?

'The practices seem designed to deliberately antagonize, frustrate and anger inmates . . . ' is appended to her statement.

And like the cameo of queuing in the rain above is another affidavit.

Approximately 3 minutes before 8, about 10 people came inside to get out of the heavy rain. They were quickly told by the staff, 'We didn't call anyone in yet, go back outside'. For 3 minutes this group of visitors had to stand out in the rain waiting for a signal from the staff while they chatted amongst themselves.

(Affidavits, 2006)

Data Sources

The Midrash Methodology gives the scholar scope to write beautifully, personally, creatively and courageously. *Beyond the Wire* includes poetry, theatre, film, prison affidavits and extant literature to support and validate the discoveries in the midrashim. The data sources of the Midrash Methodology are first personal data from the midst of living relations and shared situations, supported by, in this instance, public-domain data, including poetry, performative works, media reports and investigations, historical articles and monographs, international research material and local eye-witness accounts of the same or similar living relations and shared situations.

Phase Three

The example in this chapter illuminates the damage to visitors of asylum-seekers in detention centres who: (a) typically would not encounter the criminal–penal system and so were particularly bruised and some traumatised by the guards and the detention (prison) system as supported by the Affidavits (2006, Akhmatova, 2000, Newman and Mares, 2007); (b) visitors by association were criminalised and mostly treated with disdain, disregard and in an undignified manner by the guards when visiting detainees.

In turn, personal experiences lead to greater albeit disproportionate understanding of asylum-seekers suffering from the disregard and undignified treatment[8] meted out to them inside the detention centres. It also shows the treatment of detainees and their visitors equates to the treatment

---

8   There was a slight improvement until September 2013. Now detainees are called transferees and they are not called by their names. Reminiscent of other regimes they (men, women, and children) are called by number.

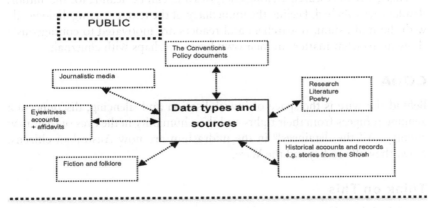

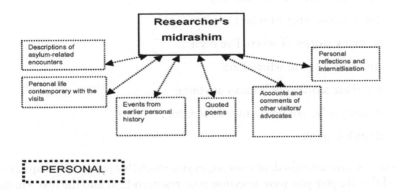

Figure 7.1 Data Sources

of convicted criminals in maximum-security jails and their visitors. The examples of numbing and treatment of the visitor are just two examples offered to in this chapter to operationalise the Midrash Methodology.

Leavy (2009) opens her book as follows: 'Many researchers in the social and behavioural sciences enter the academy full of what my mother calls "chutzpah": a palpable energy, desire to make a difference, and fearlessness about shaking things up' (p. 1). I am encouraging readers of this chapter to have 'chutzpah'. The Midrash Methodology opens the way for the researchers' passion, truth and relevancy to prevail. When Levinas was asked about the importance of science, his response supports the place of values and ethics in research and knowledge formation. 'I do not underestimate the importance of knowledge[9] but I do not consider it to be the ultimate axiological judgement' (Levinas, 1984).

9 In this context Levinas is referring to scientific or positivist knowledge.

This genre of research-writing energises and can be healing for the author. Readers are touched. Feeling the immediacy of the text, engaging dialogically with the midrashim, researchers and readers are motivated to courageously show up to what matters in their own lives – perhaps with chutzpah.

CODA

Behind the wire is the space of invisibilisation and silencing, disconnecting genuine refugees from their rights and their humanity in the eyes of their new country. All the detainees[10] in the midrashim are now Australian citizens. Now, they all are Beyond the Wire.

Think on This

All of these lines across my face

Tell you the story of who I am

So many stories of where I've been

And how I got to where I am

But these stories don't mean anything

When you've got no on to tell them to. . . .

Brandi Carlisle

If you are now energised, or curious, as you reach this page, or perhaps as you read this chapter you were inserting your research field into the text – instead of asylum-seekers – would you know how to start using the methodology?

Perhaps simply you would like to incorporate the Midrash Methodology into your current or next research project.

What would you include from your existing research data?

If you were starting a project how would you know that Midrash Methodology was best suited to the research on hand?

What research opportunity does this chapter open up for you?

If you already have collected data my suggestion is to read your data and then put it away. Transport yourself back to the environment where you were gathering your information. Bring to mind the subjects, the place or the computer surveys (whatever method of gathering you used). Begin writing a midrash by re-membering your experience at that time. Allow phenomenological multidimensional, multimodal memories to come. Use your physical, olfactory and kinesthetic senses to clue your memories to the surface. As you write check all your senses in the present moment as well. Your body knows

---

10 Detainees' names have been changed.

and communicates if you listen. Your brain knows what must be told. Use intuition too.

Re-read *The Windmills of My Mind: My Story Becomes Midrash* (above). Trust yourself. The existing data will lead you to different midrashim.

If, however, you are beginning a new project, write the midrashim as the method of gathering data as described in this chapter.

Follow the iterative steps as a hermeneutic.

As with all writing, you'll find your voice – that is, if you choose passion, fire in your belly and a good dose of chutzpah!

References

Affidavits 2006. Disrespectful Treatment At The Intake Center. In: EYE, A. (ed.) Caught! The Public list of judicial misconduct, prosecutorial misconduct, ethics violations, civil rights violations and legal misconduct in Rhode Island. Rhode Island: The Intake Service Center (ISC) is a maximum security facility which serves as Rhode Island's jail for male offenders.

Agamben, G. 1998. *Homo Sacer: Sovereign Power and Bare Life*, Stanford, CA, Stanford University Press.

Akhmatova, A. 2000. *Rekviem*, Moscow, Vagruis.

Arendt, H. 1948. The concentration camps. *Partisan Reviews*, 15(7), 743–763.

Becker, C. 1992. *Living and Relating: An Introduction to Phenomenology*, Thousand Oaks, CA, Sage.

Buber, M. 1958. *I and Thou*, New York, Charles Scribner's Sons.

Csikszentmihalyi, M. 2008. *Flow: The Psychology of Optimal Experience*, New York, Harper Perenniel Modern Classics.

Denzin, N. and Lincoln, Y. 2003. *The Handbook of Qualitative Research*, Thousand Oaks, CA, Sage Publications.

Gadamer, H.-G. 1979. *Truth and Method*, London, Continuum Publishing Group.

Kafle, N. P. 2011. Hermeneutic phenomenological research method simplified. *Bodhi: An Interdisciplinary Journal*, 5, 181–200.

Kepnes, S. 1992. *The Text as Thou*, Bloominton, IN, Indiana University Press.

Leavy, P. 2009. *Method Meet Art: Arts Based Research Practice*, New York, Guilford Press.

Levinas, E. 1961. *Totality and Infinity*, Pennyslvania, PA, Duquesne University Press.

Levinas, E. 1984. *Is it Righteous to Be? Interviews with Emmanuel Levinas*, Stanford, CA, Stanford University Press.

Newman, L. and Mares, S. (eds) 2007. *Acting from the Heart: Australian Advocates for Asylum Seekers Tell Their Stories*, Sydney, Finch.

Reinharz, S. 1992. *Feminist Methods in Social Research*, Boston, MA, Oxford University Press.

Van Manen, M. 1990. *Researching Lived Experience: Human Science for an Action Sensitive Pedagogy*, New York, State Univeristy of New York Press.

Wainer, D. 2015. *Beyond the Wire: Levinas vis-à-vis Villawood*, Cronulla, Australia, Book Boffin.

Wilcke, M. M. 2006. Hermeneutic phenomenology as a research method in social work. *Currents: New Scholarship in the Human Services*, 1, 10.

Index

For Product Safety Concerns and Information please contact our
EU representative GPSR@taylorandfrancis.com Taylor & Francis
Verlag GmbH, Kaufingerstraße 24, 80331 München, Germany